The Emerging Leader

Ways to a Stronger Team

Dean Tjosvold
Mary M. Tjosvold

LEXINGTON BOOKS
An Imprint of Macmillan, Inc.

NEW YORK

Maxwell Macmillan Canada
TORONTO

Maxwell Macmillan International
NEW YORK   OXFORD   SINGAPORE   SYDNEY

Library of Congress Cataloging-in-Publication Data

Tjosvold, Dean.
    The emerging leader : ways to a stronger team / Dean Tjosvold, Mary M. Tjosvold.
        p.   cm.
    Includes bibliographical references and index.
    ISBN 0-02-932595-1
    1. Leadership. 2. Work groups. I. Tjosvold, Mary M. II. Title.
HD57.7.T56   1993   93-21690
658.4'036—dc20   CIP

Lexington Books
An Imprint of Macmillan, Inc.
866 Third Avenue, New York, N. Y. 10022

Maxwell Macmillan Canada, Inc.
1200 Eglinton Avenue East
Suite 200
Don Mills, Ontario M3C 3Nl

Macmillan, Inc. is part of the Maxwell Communication Group of Companies.

Printed in the United States of America

printing number
1   2   3   4   5   6   7   8   9   10

To the people of Camilia Rose,
Margaret Place, DeMar, Outreach/Six Acres,
etc by design, and Mary T. Associates,
who support our learning to lead

Contents

Part Four

Deepening Competence
Continuous Development

Preface

The Emerging Leader is for people who want to learn how to lead
their task forces, departments, and organizations to be more lively,
adaptive, and effective. Leaders and people who aspire to be leaders feel an urgency to create new ways of working to serve customers. Tired of putting out fires and struggling through crises,
they want to develop organizations of value, credibility, and
longevity.

True leaders are willing to begin with themselves. Confronting
their blind spots and building on their strengths, they strive for
ongoing personal development. They reach out to others as they
ask others to reach out. They create an environment where people
can help each other be effective and learn.

Leaders appreciate that they and their organizations confront a
serious challenge: to learn how to change, or else to be the pawn
of change. A customer today is not necessarily one tomorrow; an
efficient way of working now is not necessarily efficient in the
future; success this year does not guarantee success next year.
Companies that have been celebrated for their organizational
excellence one year must restructure and downsize a few years
later. Organizations need ongoing revitalization, and people need
continual development in order to succeed in this rapidly changing
era. Leaders find security in working together to innovate and
improve, not in maintaining the false hope of finding an island free
from change.

We often blame change and thereby give it the power to disrupt
and destroy. But rapid change is a messenger. The need to adapt

and learn continually has always been real. The pace of contemporary change has only made holding on to the illusion of a stable status quo less tenable and more dangerous.

No one is simply "born" knowing how to unite a group behind a common vision and foster the spirited exchange necessary to adapt to change and empower people to deliver quality service. Many people who have been successful throughout their careers suddenly stumble when they are promoted to leadership positions. Developing the sensitivities and capacities to lead is a lifelong pursuit, not a one- or two-step process.

The Emerging Leader offers a research-based, action-oriented plan for learning how to lead. Leaders can use these guidelines to analyze situations, decide how to act, and reflect and learn from their experiences.

The Book's Agenda

Leaders are not omnipotent and are not the sole reason for the success of their teams. But they are critical for productive, innovative organizations. Leaders know that through these organizations individuals find fulfillment and develop their abilities, and companies earn the respect and the continuing business of their customers.

The Emerging Leader provides concrete ideas and procedures that you can use to develop your leadership abilities. The four parts of the book describe the core steps to becoming a leader. Part One focuses on leading as a way of developing productive relationships. Leaders often get distracted by the myth that they should single-handedly turn companies around and by pressure on them to get tasks done and meet deadlines. However, developing productive relationships is the essential leadership role that has a long-term impact on teams and organizations.

Part Two discusses the importance of understanding cooperation and competition. Productive relationships are supportive and affirming, yet also confronting and demanding. Cooperation theory reconciles these characteristics into a coherent approach to effective relationships.

Part Three shows how to apply the theory of cooperation to

meet job challenges and strengthen leadership abilities. To learn about cooperative relationships and how to develop them requires action, experience, and reflection.

Part Four, finally, shows the need to commit to ongoing development. Leadership is a journey, not a destination. Leaders continually learn as they meet new challenges. They enlist their teams and organizations to support the learning of everyone.

The Emerging Leader shows leaders and followers alike how they can apply cooperation theory to work together as an effective team. Reading and experimenting with cooperation theory will not give leaders and employees instant success. However, this book offers the experiences and discussions they can use to learn how to lead and work as a team. After using *The Emerging Leader* to help you strengthen your competence and confidence, you can use our *Leading the Team Organization: How to Create an Enduring Competitive Advantage* (Lexington Books, 1991) to lead a transformation of your organization. *Leading the Team Organization* shows how to change a whole organization and foster productive teamwork throughout the organization.

The Give-and-Take of Leading

The glorification of leaders is a roadblock to learning to lead. Would-be leaders feel intimidated and skeptical that they can ever meet overly idealistic expectations of them. Debates about whether leaders are born or made and about whether the person or the situation results in leadership make leading seem general and abstract. But leadership is very much an everyday thing. It is part of the give and take of social life.

Tom Peters has advised, "Read more novels and fewer business books: relationships really are all there is." This book uses a narrative story to help you see the many faces of cooperative leadership and to illustrate how ideas developed through research can be applied in concrete situations. The people you will meet are fictitious, but they are based on real people who deal with real problems whom we have encountered as employees, managers, business owners, educators, researchers, and consultants. We hope that their confronting their challenges will give you the insight and courage to move away from divisive ways of working to become a more effective team.

Leaders take us on a journey to places we have not gone before. They give voice to our common aspirations, inspire confidence that we can overcome obstacles, and help us move forward. You are about to embark on your own journey of learning to lead. We ourselves have taken the lead to develop this book, but we can only be successful when you and your colleagues are able to use the book's ideas, guides, and story to strengthen your leadership and your organization.

PART ONE

Getting Focused
Leadership as Productive Relationships

a poor leader: the people fear
a good leader: the people love
a great leader: the people say, "we did it ourselves."
—Sun Tzu, military philosopher, fourth century B.C.

Leaders have the potential to have a long-term, significant impact on people and their organization. Yet many managers, wedded to old work habits and satisfactions of doing concrete tasks, fail to see the possibilities of creating a more innovative future. Myths and stereotypes of leadership distract and discourage them from trying to lead. They end up managing the status quo, not leading people to work more effectively and creatively.

Recognizing that it is through teamwork that jobs get done, that customers are served, and that the organization learns and adapts, leaders challenge traditional ways of working by creating productive relationships that empower people. They disavow notions that mistrustful, competitive relationships are inevitable, and they search for valid ideas about the nature of productive relationships. They commit themselves to learning to lead a team as they ask people to commit themselves to new ways of working together.

1

Learning to Think We

Of the strengths that separate us from other companies, the Number 1 thing is our teams and teamwork. We have about 1,900 teams across our group at all levels. Teamwork allows us to accomplish things better than we could do it any other way.
—Jerry Junkins, CEO, Texas Instruments
Malcom Baldridge award winner, 1992

Learning to lead is fraught with pitfalls and paralyzing images. The popular press extols charismatic individualists who overcome resistance to rescue companies single-handedly. Historians propose the great man theory of change; political scientists argue that bureaucracies overcome any attempts on the part of leaders to change them.

Perhaps the most misleading of all assumptions is that leadership is a characteristic of a person. It is a mistake to focus on the abilities and personalities of a leader or to attribute a group's success or failure to its leader alone. A leader cannot lead without followers. One who walks steadfastly down the road alone is not a leader. Leadership is done by leaders and followers together. The reasons for leadership's success or failure must be found in the relationships, in how people have worked together to accomplish their purposes.

Leadership involves the leader empowering and assisting followers as they empower her. But leadership also involves relationships among followers. How employees relate to each other very much affects both their willingness to be led and their effectiveness. A key to successful leadership is to structure and develop relationships among followers so that they empower each other. Leadership today is too complex and challenging to be left to one person; it is only successful when everyone does it together.

Sometimes leadership is trivialized as the ability to get along and keep peace. But it is much more than an outgoing manner and a quick smile. Leadership is much more, even, than the ability to work honestly and directly or to use conflict productively.

Leaders nurture an organization's relationships. They build the synergistic teamwork necessary for an organization to be flexible and vibrant and take advantage of change. Rather than managing the status quo, they lead others to feel directed, united, and empowered to accomplish their common vision.

Confronting Challenges to Leading

Managers have traditionally emphasized getting the job done, developing new products, improving marketing, and reducing costs. Contemporary leaders recognize that the advantages of these activities are increasingly fragile and short-lived. Competitors quickly develop new products, create technologies to reduce costs and improve quality, and enter profitable markets. Organizations must be able to learn and adapt if they are to remain viable.

The focus on the "learning organization" and continuous improvement has in turn begun to expose the traditional assumptions that an organization is a collection of individual specialists and workers and that the key to organizational success is to motivate each person to work harder. On these assumptions, an impersonal organizational world was expected to allow individuals to work unencumbered, without the need to discuss and coordinate. It was the manager's role to solve any coordination problems between individuals and departments.

Leaders recognize that quality team relationships are a more enduring competitive advantage. They are an organization's lifeblood, through which information flows, communication occurs, and problems are identified and solved. Spirited teamwork develops new products, reduces costs, improves quality, finds new customers, values diversity, and sets ethical standards. Leaders realize that by strengthening relationships, they have a continuing impact.

Yet merely appreciating the value of teamwork does not give managers the abilities they need to help and teach others to work together. When considering how to strengthen an organization, they may fall back onto simplistic analyses—"people need more motivation," "remove the barriers to excellence," "we need more people." They turn to ineffective actions—"set up competitive contests to motivate and add some creativity," "hand out awards to the winners." To improve synergy, they put two warring individuals under one supervisor. Less effectively, they give two warring groups their own buildings and vice-presidents.

These Band-Aid measures may have been adequate previously, but they are not now. A few years ago, U.S. automobile firms let years slip by as development and production people squabbled over new models, allowed defective cars onto the market rather than confront sloppy supervisors and hostile workers, and tried to buy industrial peace with generous wage settlements. The result was lost market share. Now, despite quicker product development, quality improvements, and more effective employee relations, U.S. auto companies must reduce costs and improve quality continually to win customers.

Developing high-quality productive relationships has become increasingly difficult. People in today's organizations must cross many boundaries and barriers to work effectively together. Organizations are more diverse as females, immigrants, and people of color increasingly enter the workforce. In geographically dispersed companies, people are expected to collaborate through telephone and fax with only occasional face-to-face meetings. They have few opportunities for informal interactions where they can feel part of an organization, find out the latest developments, and make serendipitous contributions. Specialists and professionals from different departments, organizations, countries, and cultural backgrounds are increasingly asked to collaborate.

Despite the urgency of investing continually in building effective teams, too few managers do so. Rather, they wait until people and groups are screaming at each other or not talking, and then, if funds are available, they hire a consultant to patch things up. Leaders need to take a proactive approach to help people up and down and across the organization work together fully and effectively. They need a clear focus on their mission and a valid framework to make diverse, large, dispersed, and decentralized organizations synergistic and vibrant.

Learning to Lead Together

To become leaders, managers must challenge outworn ideas of their role as taskmasters and outworn views of organizations as composed of independent individuals. They need fresh, valid models of how to lead and build successful organizations. They must put their values and ideas to work in credible, effective ways. Managers need the assistance of others to experiment with new ways of leading and learning from their experiences.

Chief executive officers report that gaining practical experience was critical for their success. Rising to the challenge of turning around a weak operation, starting from scratch, moving from a line to a staff position, and heading a task force compelled them to develop and learn. Through the fire of real challenges, they drew upon their inner resources, gained insight, and experimented with new ways of coping. Twenty years later, they vividly recall learning valuable lessons, refining their abilities, and solidifying their self-confidence. Yet other people face equally challenging situations but learn little from them.

Ideas are needed to analyze situations, determine what should be done, create plans, and inspire persistent action. With such a framework, people can use their experiences to get feedback on the usefulness of their decisions and actions. Feedback can confirm or disconfirm the ideas they used to guide their actions. Experience itself does not teach; using ideas to make use of opportunities and to reflect on experience does.

We now know that people understand ideas and learn from their experiences much more thoroughly through the rich exchange, discussion, and debate of joint learning. There are several reasons that explain the power of group learning. Mentors and colleagues model important values and effective procedures and provide the emotional support to incorporate new ideas. Several people can use their various perspectives to create plans that are appropriate and effective for a given situation. A great deal of ingenuity is needed to apply leadership ideas to fit the personalities and circumstances of situations. Individuals have blind spots that prevent them from owning up to their shortcomings. Their biases can exaggerate their successes and failures. It is easier to accept negative feedback if other people are able to help us use it to improve our abilities for the future.

Spirited teamwork means both the goal of leading and the means to learn to lead. To become a leader, managers debate ideas and explore issues with co-workers; they gather support to take courageous risks; they get feedback and suggestions from employees. This method of learning to lead reinforces the leader's message of spirited teamwork.

Cooperation Theory

Cooperation theory offers an approach that aspiring leaders can use to create productive teamwork. When people believe their goals are cooperative ("we are in this together," "we swim or sink together"), they are committed to promoting each other and to helping each other be effective ("we trust and rely upon each other"). Then they are prepared to coordinate effectively and consider each other's ideas, to try to combine them into mutually beneficial solutions. They work together to get the job done and strengthen their relationships.

In contrast, when people believe their goals are competitive ("we're in a struggle to see who wins," "if he swims, I sink"), they remain committed to promoting their own interests, but that commitment makes them want to see others perform ineffectively and fail ("we suspect each other" "we are on guard"). They find it dif-

Cooperation Theory

ficult to speak their minds, and they often frustrate each other and try to unilaterally impose solutions. Both the job and their relationships suffer.

The evidence clearly indicates that cooperative relationships between leaders and followers and among followers are the foundation for productive teamwork in organizations. (Chapter 5 describes theory and research on cooperation and competition in more detail.) When leaders and followers believe their goals go together, they use power constructively, discuss opposing views, manage conflict, learn from experiences, get the job done, and move toward their vision.

Cooperation theory is flexible enough to be applied to a wide range of situations. It can be used in a group of two or two thousand; it can be applied on the shop floor or in the executive boardroom; it can guide leadership and teamwork at universities, marketing agencies, or any workplace.

Cooperation theory is a guide, not a simplistic straitjacket. It helps leaders make decisions; it does not give them a script to perform. When leaders and followers understand the nature of cooperative relationships, they can structure new ways to work together. As they learn more about the theory, they find multiple ways to apply it and incorporate other approaches. Learning to lead with cooperation theory is an ongoing effort, not something to be pushed aside when a new slogan appears.

Using cooperation theory gives much, but it requires much too. It takes creativity to apply it to concrete situations, and it requires persistence to acquire the skills to use it. We will see in the next chapters people working together to overcome barriers to focus on the mission of leaders and to understand and use cooperation theory to lead.

2

To Do Something or For Something to Do

Soon after the completion of Disney World, someone said, "Isn't it too bad Walt Disney didn't live to see this." I replied, "He did see it. That's why it's here."
—Mike Vance, creative director, Walt Disney Studios

"Why did I take this stupid job?" Dr. Graham Welsch moaned as he sat down with Nora, his wife, before dinner one evening. "Everyone growls and complains all day long. I thought I was tired of hearing patients complain, but at least they listen when you tell them something."

Nora was concerned; she even felt guilty when Graham got so frustrated. After all, she had encouraged him to accept the position as director of Cedar Lake Clinic of Health East—a network of clinics run by the Weber Foundation—though she was surprised when he had. Recently, Graham had become very outspoken about his frustrations with the job. Nora welcomed his complaints, though, since they were much easier to live with than the sullenness and withdrawal that were his tendency.

Recognizing that Graham had indirect ways of telling her what was bothering him, she encouraged him to talk: "I thought my office was filled with grumblers and gossipers, but your people really get into it." Nora had been a manager in a successful consumer products company for five years.

"The wonderful world of health care," Graham said. "We're supposed to be such caring people. Perhaps we give so much to our patients that we just don't have anything left over for each other."

"Though I'm in the cutthroat business of consumer products," Nora replied, "sometimes I think your people are tougher and more competitive."

"I've got news," Graham announced. "I'm going to a leadership workshop at the university for a week. It's supposed to be good. Heaven knows I could use some better handles on how to manage these people."

"That's great, honey. You can study leadership with the clinic in mind. Best of all, you can talk with other people who are in similar situations. How come you don't sound that excited?"

Graham got up to set Nora and himself a drink. "Sometimes this organization does strange things," he mused when he returned. "I was telling Derek about the workshop, and he said he heard that Colin was being sent to a three-week management program back east."

Nora now knew what was bothering Graham. She tried to sound matter-of-fact: "Good for Colin. They must expect big things from him if they put him on the fast track."

"And not so big things from me."

"Don't get down on yourself." Nora wanted to support her husband, but she didn't like—even resented—self-pity. "You know Colin has always wanted to move up the organization. You're only just beginning to show an interest in management."

"It rubs me the wrong way that some people should be given so much and the rest of us relatively little."

"I think it also rubs you the wrong way that Colin was selected," Nora observed.

"Why top management would want to put someone like Colin on the fast track who cares so little about patient care and so much about himself is beyond me!" Graham exclaimed.

"But Colin unambiguously wants to be a manager," Nora said. "Your boss might be surprised if he found out that you wanted three weeks of management development."

"It's helping patients that counts," Graham said defensively. "I've never been that interested in power-grabbing and putting myself above other people."

Nora also didn't like it, though she did not know quite why, when her husband described himself in selfless terms. "That's an old way of looking at managing. Good leaders don't grab power. They empower people."

Graham was simmering less about Colin now, but he suddenly found another hot spot. "I didn't know that taking this job would change so much for me. I'm forever running from here to there, talking, cajoling, arguing, sometimes even laughing—there's so much commotion. Funny thing is, I like it. But on days like this I wonder what it all means and whether it's worth feeling so exhausted at night."

"You could go back to dealing with patients. You're good at it," Nora suggested.

"I miss the feeling that at the end of the day I can look at my appointment book and believe that I helped real people get a little healthier. But I don't want to go back to full-time practice."

"The change was a good one for you. It was time for you to move on, I think."

"But I'm on much firmer ground when I'm treating patients. We know our job is to help patients get well. And we have some proven procedures and a lot of science behind us."

"Leadership can be fuzzy, but for some patients you weren't sure what was wrong, and some of them you couldn't help."

"That's reassuring in a strange way. But now, in managing the clinic, I feel like I'm operating without a map—just winging it. That's not a good feeling for a doctor. We like to know we're right."

"It's hard to be right as a manager." Nora hadn't thought about it before, but she had learned that trying to be right didn't help her manage. "If I had some right answers, I'd tell you. Mostly I know what not to do."

"It should be easier to manage in your operation," Graham pointed out. "Everyone knows the goal is to make money, and then everyone pulls together. We have a bunch of prima donnas, and one group fighting another, and no one thinks that they have to worry about the clinic's money. All hell will break loose when they hear I have to start cutting the budget."

Nora and Graham were only beginning to compare realistically their organizations. Before that, they had accepted the stereotypes about the vast differences between health care and consumer products organizations. Nora said, "Perhaps we're not quite so extreme and are more willing to give and take. But we have our prima donnas too. Marketing researchers, production technicians—just about everyone is a professional these days, and they all think they're right."

"We must have you beat on that score. People are so self-centered and so narrow minded," Graham lamented. "I didn't realize before I took this job how people are so into themselves. They have such educated, complex ways of expressing themselves, but all I hear is me, me, me."

"Change them so that they work as a team. You *did* ask why you took the job."

"Right," Graham said sardonically. "I suppose you want me to use those words in our philosophy statement about 'working together' and 'cooperation.' I can hear them laughing at me and talking behind my back about who suckered Graham this time. They're suspicious of all slogans, especially management ones. These are tough-minded people who went into health care because they didn't want to be managed."

"You'll have to welcome them to the real world," Nora said, "where they do work in an organization and must be managed, and where their suspicion and divisiveness really get in the way."

"What I think needs to happen is that they all have to remember they were hired and get paid to take care of patients and fulfil our contracts. They must realize that this is a business and that we need revenue. These people think money comes out of the sky."

"Money *has* come out of the sky, for years." Nora laughs.

"That's an illusion."

"I can see why they don't want to give up this illusion and start to think they have to earn money by serving their customers. But we have professionals like that too. We're trying to get them to think that they're part of the business, to think like business people."

"That's just what people in health care don't want to do," Graham said. "We think we're way above business and the corporate world."

"It's a special business, to be sure." Nora was getting annoyed because they seemed to be going around in circles. "What do you want to do? That's the question. Knowing you, you'll want to have accomplished something when you're finished. It won't be enough just to be busy."

Graham had some ideas: He wanted the clinic to be more respected in the professional community and to mesh patient care and research more successfully. He knew that organizations needed to manage diversity and incorporate ethical decision making. He also wanted, though he couldn't put it into words, people in the clinic to be grateful to him. He was embarrassed to talk about his hopes, even with his wife. "To leave the place better than when I began," he finally said.

"I thought you were going to say something about not making the clinic worse, like the first rule of treating patients."

"That's true too."

"You might need something more specific." Nora smiled. "Then everyone in the department would know why you took the job. Let's talk later. I think the kids have dinner ready."

Caught in the Status Quo Cycle

Graham was becoming committed to being a leader. He was involved in the give-and-take and the emotional ups and downs of managing. Although the traditional image of managing is dispassionate analysis and decision making and exercising power to control subordinates, the reality of managing is ongoing meetings, crises, and conflicts. Managers do work with and through other people.

Yet Graham and many other managers got so caught up in their daily activities that the long-term purpose and impact of their work gets lost. High achievers, they enjoyed getting important tasks completed. They found the adrenaline excitement in dealing with crises, both exhilarating and exhausting. At the end of the week, feeling drained and stressed, they were assured that they had used their abilities, been needed, and fulfilled their mandate to keep the group moving.

But rather than leading, they were actually managing the status quo. They were taking care of immediate matters, getting jobs done, and keeping the bureaucracy going. They were not leading their groups on journeys to where they had not gone before. They were not helping their groups be more effective and innovative for the long term.

The Cedar Lake Clinic's failure to develop high-quality, cooperative relationships lay behind Graham's predicament. Because people in different areas of the clinic did not seek each other out, he had to cajole and encourage them to meet to discuss joint projects and find effective ways of sharing technology and other resources. Unable to deal with their conflicts themselves, Graham was being pushed into the role of intermediary to channel communication and arbitrate disputes. Because employees did not complain directly to their supervisors about their frustrations, small groups of them formed to press their demands on the clinic. General meetings were busy and superficial because Graham and his peers were unable to confront their differences publicly.

A persistent and pernicious impact of such impersonal, conflict-avoidance relationships is that they make it difficult for a person like Graham to get committed to changing them. In this situation ineffective communication and conflict are so prevalent that they seemed natural and immutable. Plans to change them seem so pie-in-the-sky that Graham does not take them seriously. The language of "cooperation" and "working together" is not only distant and unreal but insulting. People feel they are being unfairly criticized for not living up to an impractical ideal. They dismiss research about leadership and relationships as soft and unscientific.

These nonconfrontive relationships undermine any process of change. Even if he had been committed to developing more productive relationships, Graham would have found it awkward to turn to his colleagues for advice, support, and encouragement to make the clinic more into a team. Indeed, he worried that people would snicker at his näiveté if he suggested that they needed to work better by working together. People at the clinic found it difficult and exhausting even to discuss conflicts over tasks, much less to confront the emotional issue of their mistrustful relationships. They were unskilled and uncomfortable at mutual problem solving and managing their feelings.

It is understandable that a manager like Graham looked for a quick fix. Perhaps if everyone talked about and became committed to quality, they might come to think people would work together and mistrust would disappear. Perhaps scheduling more meetings would improve communication, or perhaps fewer meetings would dissolve conflict.

At this point, asking the people at the Cedar Lake Clinic to build their relationships would be to play to their weakness, not to their strengths. Graham and his staff would be asking them to do what they were not very good at. Instead, they preferred to treat patients and to complete tasks about which they felt confident and comfortable.

Breaking Away

Graham was frustrated as well as exhilarated by these ongoing battles. As a doctor, he had once taken solace in the fact that he was at least trying to do something unquestionably useful, even if he was not always successful in helping patients get well. Now he wondered what the value was of managing and getting through a crisis, only to face another crisis. He had real doubt that his work was a long-term contribution.

The people at the clinic were also injured by their competitive, conflict-avoiding relationships. They held their grievances inside themselves and gossiped and complain because discussing their frustrations directly with the perpetrators is too risky. When they did deal directly with protagonists, conflict often escalated, leaving them feeling even more powerless and hostile. They held grudges and thought of themselves as superior, but at the same time they regretted not having the respect and friendship of their rivals.

The clinic lost out, too, because people were not working as a team. It was unable to respond to challenges and to take advantage of opportunities. Poor coordination undermined the quality of the care it provided and increased costs. Specialists continued to address problems from their traditional perspectives rather than engage in interdisciplinary research. People were unprepared to make specific, persuasive recommendations about how to reduce the budget, leaving top management to feel it had no option but to make blunt, across-the-board cuts.

These ineffective relationships were important barriers to confronting and improving how the clinic people worked together. They had to be changed. But only true leaders can act as catalysts to create the necessary change.

Leadership begins when one challenges the status quo and helps people to invest in their relationships so that the group and organization become more innovative and adaptive. Leaders describe a better possible way of working in concrete, realistic terms, making people knowledgeable and confident about how they can improve their relationships. Rather than tell people what to do, leaders galvanize and guide their collective action for ongoing improvement. Leadership is not something a manager does to or for employees but is what the leader and employees do together to strengthen their teamwork and collective work.

Leadership demanded that Graham reach out to the people in the clinic. But it is also required Graham to look inward to know his own aspirations, values, and capabilities. People want to follow managers they know, trust, and respect. To lead requires communicating who one is as a person and articulating one's hopes and plans.

Although leading requires much, it does not require perfection. Rather, the leader shows that she and others can learn from mistakes and experiences together and become an effective team. Credibility is based on honest discussion and joint work, not on illusions of perfection and infallibility. In the next chapters, we will see Graham working with Nora and others to learn how to develop his leadership abilities and to build productive relationships in the clinic.

To Do Something

Guides for Action

- Seek ways you can have a long-term impact.
- Examine your current leadership approach.
- Talk about your leadership concerns with supporters.
- Understand that you can make a difference by helping others make a difference.
- Commit yourself to learning to lead a team.

Pitfalls to Avoid

- Getting caught up in getting tasks done.
- Equating being busy with being an effective leader.
- Suppressing your feelings of having little long-term impact.
- Redoubling your efforts when you are feeling ineffective, to avoid reflecting on your leadership approach.
- Relying on quick fixes to improve how people work together.

3

Searching for Leadership

The secret to success is to stay in love. Staying in love gives you the fire to really ignite other people, to see inside other people, to have a greater desire to get things done than other people. A person who is not in love doesn't really feel the kind of excitement that helps them to get ahead and lead others and to achieve. I don't know any other fire, any other thing in life that is more exhilarating and is more positive a feeling than love is.
—Army Major General John H. Stanford, in The Leadership Challenge, *James M. Kouzes & Barry Z. Posner*

"This may be a long week," Graham muttered to himself as the leadership workshop began. He had become distracted with work, but driving to the workshop he had been hopeful that he could learn something important and valuable here. But he was also cautious and hesitant. Was it realistic to think that someone could teach him leadership? Would he have to put up with a eccentric professor who knows only about theories of leadership and put him through strange activities? The workshop's opening seemed to confirm his fears, not his hopes.

Richard Fielding, the professor who had developed and run the workshop for ten summers, seemed too ambivalent and weak to know much about leadership. He talked vaguely about the need for "transformational" leaders who changed the basic direction of their organizations, and about corporate cultures that needed paradigm shifts. How was that going to help Graham?

In fact, Richard did feel ambivalent. He liked working with actual managers—it's a change of pace from teaching students, and it kept him in touch with the world of work and gave him a feeling of having an impact. Yet he found managers unpredictable. A few summers, they had turned against him and grumbled and complained that the workshop was old-fashioned, not cutting-edge enough.

Richard had made the workshop more basic and relaxed over the years. The first few times he gave the course, he had crammed in many facts and theories. He had made it like his MBA course, only more intense. But he had come to appreciate that what is crucial for leadership development is something more intangible and basic than knowing about leadership theories and research on paper. He recognized, too, that the networking parts of the workshop—participants getting to know other participants, talking over issues during coffee breaks, and keeping in touch with each other after the workshop—were very valuable, perhaps more valuable than the content. Somehow he wanted *how* he was teaching to be congruent with *what* he was teaching.

Yet he knew he was violating the managers' expectations of a fast-paced, fully packed, "don't waste my time" course. These were adrenline-filled managers who enjoyed, even took refuge in action and challenges. He knew that high-status workshops usually demanded that managers work night and day on papers and cases. The "customers" seemed to want to work hard; when they did, they felt that the programs was giving them what they wanted. When they were working hard, the managers didn't have time to evaluate and criticize what they were learning.

Though sometimes Richard wished he could just give in, he had become committed to challenging the managers' expectations and to getting them to appreciate the value of thoughtful reflection, of getting together with their peers to critique what they are learning, and to talk about themselves and their situations. He wanted them to evolve from hard-charging managers to true leaders.

When Richard tried to get the group involved in discussing the nature of effective leaders, Graham kept quiet and wondered why Richard did not just summarize what was already known. A few participants seemed to have already been to a leadership workshop, for they easily talked about "empowerment," "taking the organization on a journey," and "spirited teamwork."

Soon, though, Graham got involved. Richard gave them a short lecture on the distributed theory of leadership. Leaders have two major functions: promoting tasks and promoting people. They exercise *task leadership* by identifying a problem, presenting and asking for information about it, and summarizing progress in solving it. They exercise *people leadership* by encouraging participation, contributing to a warm climate, and managing conflict. Half the workshop participants practice these behaviors in small work groups, while the other half watched and gave them feedback.

The observers concluded that people at the workshop were much more tuned in to task leadership than people leadership. The woman observing Graham told him that she had seen him perform only two people leadership behaviors of encouraging participation, but fourteen behaviors directly related to getting a task done.

Graham, like other managers, argued that the situation called for task leadership. There were no personal issues or conflicts that needed their attention; they had to focus on the job. Richard, however, had videotaped the group. The video showed very concretely how uncomfortable and anxious people had been with each other. They tapped their feet, rubbed their hands, and pulled their hair. They had serious facial expressions, worked hard to break in to make a comment, and did not build upon each other's contributions. By this point, Richard had captured Graham's full attention.

At the end of the day, Richard divided the participants into groups of three to discuss what they had learned and what they wanted to learn the rest of the week. He made sure that the groups were made up of people who did not know each other and who worked for diverse firms.

"I'm an engineer in the sewage business," Maureen introduced herself to the surprised laughter of Graham and Serge, the other members of their group. "If you live within the metropolitan area, then you're our customer and we take care of you."

"I hope you appreciate our business," Serge deadpanned.

"We do, but it's hard for us to show it." Maureen smiled back.

"Do you all need more leadership?" Graham asked. "Seems to me that you're in a dependable, steady market. All this stuff about how things are changing so rapidly and how leaders must transform organizations doesn't seem that relevant."

"From the outside, I can see how we might look like that, but there are big changes in the sewage business. We have much higher standards but reduced budgets. As people become more knowledgeable and concerned about the environment, they place new demands on us, especially on regulating industrial discharge. We need change. We do need leadership."

After Graham explained his situation, Serge told how his family construction company was under great pressure. "Construction has always been up and down, but we have more problems than just a slowdown. We drive customers away; it's getting so that people don't want to build their own homes. They just don't have the time and patience to work with us anymore. Our workforce seems more transitory, and less dependable too. All kinds of things are making business and our lives hard. If this weren't a third-generation company, I might sell out and try something else."

Over the following days of the workshop, Graham and others stayed involved. In discussing "contingency leadership" theories, they learned to appreciate that, since there is no one best leadership style, leaders should not rigidly fix on one style but must act in ways that are appropriate and effective for the situation. They debated whether democratic leaders are more effective than autocratic ones. They discussed the potential and the pitfalls of group problem solving. On the fourth day, they took roles in a business simulation game in which they had to work under pressure. On the fifth and last day, they got feedback from each other on their behavior during the business game and reflected on the week and what they had learned.

During the workshop, Graham, Maureen, and Serge had shared their aspirations and fears, discussed their strengths and weaknesses, and given each other feedback. They had enjoyed their discussions and camaraderie. They eagerly undertook their task of reflecting on what they had learned over the week.

"The week confirmed to me the importance of relationships and people leadership," Maureen began. "Because of our boss, we do quite a bit of that in our shop. But it's still hard for us managers to really be leaders of people."

Graham and Serge agreed. During the daylong simulation, they had many opportunities to exercise people leadership, but they were still much more tuned in to task leadership.

"People make any organization go, and we as leaders need to nurture them," Graham said. "Important, basic, yet still hard to do."

They again debated the contingency approach to leadership. "We're supposed to be flexible and use the approach that is appropriate," Serge said. "I can see that, but actually deciding which approach we should use is not that simple. Most of those theories give us rather complicated procedures for deciding which style to use. I can't see myself making such calculations."

"And we're supposed to be ourselves at the same time," Graham added.

"We should be credible too," Maureen said. "Our people must trust us, and part of that is because we are consistent and can be relied upon."

They discussed how to resolve the apparent contradiction between consistency and flexibility. They decided they needed to be consistent in their vision, ethics, and values, but within these parameters, their behavior would be flexible. "We must always be there for our employees, but sometimes we have to be soft and sometimes tough," Maureen summarized.

There was good cheer, even a festive mood as the workshop drew to a close. Richard was forthcoming in admitting that the week may have given them more questions than answers: "We've talked about some specific theories and issues and perhaps a few techniques. But I agree with the general sentiment that we have mostly focused on developing more of a leadership perspective. If you see yourself today more as a leader who develops people, and if you are thinking more as a leader rather than as a technical specialist, as someone who works with and through people rather than gets things done directly, then I'm delighted. It may not be profound, but it's a lesson too few managers learn."

Graham still felt good about the workshop, the people he met, and himself as he pulled into his driveway. He looked forward to talking to Nora about it, yet he thought it might be difficult to put it all into words for her.

"It was good," Graham said as he kissed and hugged Nora. "The workshop leader had some good points. But you're right—the best part was meeting other managers and seeing their situations."

"Great, honey. Just great." Nora had been relieved when Graham mentioned on the phone during the week that he was enjoying the workshop. Sometimes Graham could turn critical and hostile to people and ideas outside medicine.

"I had a good chance to talk about my situation and see that others have similar problems, though in different situations. A very nice, open group," he said.

"It's amazing," Nora marveled. "Get managers away from their own operations and people, and they can be so open and forthcoming. But in their own company, no one seems to have time and energy for others. Everyone wants to be right, and so there's so much suspicion."

"True. People wondered why so few managers wanted to create such open organizations as we had in the workshop," Graham said.

"Good question. Why?"

"Richard said that it wasn't so much that managers don't want to, as that they don't know how."

"Sounds like he was good."

"I had doubts about him early on, but I give him credit." Graham explained his first reactions and how later he came to appreciate Richard's relaxed, accepting style, his getting them involved and talking to each other, and how he had them work with each other and build their relationships.

"He can even lead," Nora remarked.

"Surprisingly, he turned out to be a good leader—at least, for a workshop. Now I have a better feel for what a leader does and know some jargon, but I doubt I can actually do it. I know I want to be more participative, more of a people leader, but I'm very fuzzy about how to actually do it. It is a little depressing just thinking about it."

"Rome wasn't built in a day. You can't expect one week to transform you into a seasoned leader. It takes time. It takes patience." Nora knew she had given him this lecture many times before, but she was convinced that Graham needed to hear it again.

Graham might have brushed her warning off, as he had many times before. But the workshop had left him more open, and less evaluative. These were fresh feelings for Graham, and he wanted to keep them. "Good point. I guess I can be tough on myself and too demanding."

"Enjoy yourself. Have fun. Be yourself. Surely that's part of being a leader," Nora continued.

"It's nice that I can count on you." Graham felt a rush that he had said something that he had felt many times but expressed very infrequently. Still, he could not be content. "I wish I could count on the people at Cedar Lake too," he said.

"That will take time" Nora warned. "Afterall, we've been talking and building our own relationship for many years. The people at Cedar Lake have done very little of that."

Barriers to Taking a Leader's Perspective

Graham was learning that leaders nurture people and their organizations. They help people focus on the challenge or task ahead of them, but rather than work directly on the task itself, they build the capabilities and confidence of people so that they can all be successful. Still, Graham and many others managers found it difficult to accept and put this leadership perspective into practice. Their organizations promoted them mainly because of their task abilities, seldom because of their potential for leading people.

People who are promoted into management are typically skilled and motivated to perform their jobs well and get things done. They have been excellent engineers, award-winning sales representatives, or productive technicians. Trained in a profession, they have spent years developing their competence, and they take great satisfaction in exercising it. The same strong task orientation that has led to their success, however, can be their undoing as a manager.

Once they become a manager, they have two jobs; one as technician, and one as manager. They feel more pressure to work harder and longer on tasks. They fear their boss will hold them the most accountable if their department does not perform well. They expect themselves to be able to do tasks better than anyone they supervise. They are to be a model, an example to their employees. As they ask their employees to work hard, they feel it would be hypocritical if they themselves did not stay late and be the last one to leave the office.

Leadership requires intellectual and emotional sophistication.

Many managers lack a conceptual framework for planning how to work with even a single person, much less a group of people. They may try to delegate tasks but be unable to follow up when a job is completed unsatisfactorily. If they finally muster the courage to confront a nonperforming employee, they may well conclude that the discussion was too painful and unproductive to attempt again. In the short term, it seems easier to them to do it themselves, to reassign the task, or to work around the employee in some other way.

Not only are many new managers unprepared for the rigors of leadership, they are often reluctant to change and experiment. They fear being embarrassed if they try new strategies. Might not employees laugh at them if they ask them to develop a vision and work as a team? They are supposed to be highly competent and effective. How can they risk actions that may expose them? They might lose credibility and respect and thereafter be crippled as leaders.

Underlying these difficulties is the competitive-individualistiic corporate culture that dominates many organizations today. In addition to getting jobs done, managers have been oriented toward promoting themselves and showing that they are more hard-working, more loyal, and more correct than their colleagues. Indeed, they may well be correct to believe that they were promoted into management because they won and showed their superiority. Those who are unpromoted are left to believe that they lost in the competition.

Managers often are unable to change the competitive orientation of their department and their relationships within it. Such a climate frustrates collective effort and stymies their learning to be leaders.

Experimenting with Leadership

As Graham confronted the obstacles to a leader perspective, the workshop had helped him see the fundamental value of promoting people and relationships and his special role in that important endeavor. Before the workshop, he had focused on getting the job done and somehow thought that the people side of an organization would take care of itself. He now knew he was so programmed to work on tasks that it would take a lot of effort and experimenting to change.

He thought that nurturing people might make the clinic a better place to work and might help him feel more effective. Perhaps investing in people is a strategy that he as a leader could tap. He was both exhilarated by these challenges and uncertain he could meet them.

Graham was also learning how to learn. He realized that learning is a collaborative effort. Reading and reflection by himself would not have led to the insights he had gotten at the workshop. It was through discussing basic ideas, listening to others talk about their leadership challenges, and getting feedback and support that Graham began to understand leadership. Graham was also learning how much he depended upon Nora's encouragement to reflect on his situation and get perspective. His appreciation of group learning would, as we will see, help Graham experiment with new ways to lead.

Graham was at the beginning. He had some basic confusions about the leader role that made him uncertain and unwilling to experiment. He needed a more integrated set of ideas that would guide his leadership. In the next chapter, we will see how Graham came to appreciate that developing quality relationships would help him promote people and productivity and become a leader.

Searching for Leadership

Guides for Action

- Develop a support group to help you challenge old, competitive ways of working.
- Debate and discuss leadership with others.
- Use feedback to examine your leadership style.
- Recognize the need for people leadership as well as task leadership.
- Focus on the vision of empowering people.

- Experiment with new ways of creating more productive relationships.
- Enjoy the journey of learning to lead.

Pitfalls to Avoid

- Focusing solely on getting tasks done.
- Relying on your technical skills to be an effective leader.
- Equating being a leader with working longer and harder.
- Searching for the one way of behaving that is appropriate for all situations.
- Eschewing a vision for your leadership because of the need to be flexible.
- Trying to be a leader by yourself.
- Allowing competitive and independent ways of working to frustrate your learning to lead.

4

Leadership as Teamwork

The primary efforts of leaders need to be directed to the maintenance and guidance of organizations as whole systems of activities. I believe this to be the most distinctive and characteristic leadership behavior, but it is the least obvious and least understood.
—*Chester Barnard, early management theorist*

"I'm trying to do the right thing," Graham said impatiently. A few weeks had passed, and the strain was beginning to drain him of the goodwill and cheer he had the week after the workshop. Yet he felt his learning from the workshop had stood him in good stead and was making a significant if perhaps not widely noticed difference in his handling of clinic employees. He was pleased that he had been supportive as well as firm of a nurse named Vicki Hall. Yet now he was showing his annoyance more than he usually allowed himself to with Carlos Santiago, who as the manager of the department of medicine was the head physician.

"I'll tell you one more time, Graham," Carlos said. "It's clear that she goofed. She didn't perform the mandatory task of giving a tetanus shot. Everyone knows to do that. We've got standards to maintain here."

"I agree, and I had a good talk with her about it," Graham replied. "I think she knows she made a mistake, and I'm convinced that she won't do it again. The finger's blood vessel, nerve, and tendon were all severed, the little girl was screaming, and Vicki had to arrange for emergency surgery." Graham wanted to say more, but he didn't want to overreact and alienate Carlos either.

"We're just lucky that Cliff asked the girl if the shot hurt her," Carlos growled. "There's a problem here with the nurses: They're getting more lax and harder to work with. We're going to lose doctors and patients around here unless the nurses smarten up."

"I don't think we want to exaggerate the problem, Carlos. We have some very good nurses here. You yourself helped us recruit some of them." Graham didn't want Carlos to move into his default mode of blaming the nurses either. As an administrator, Graham had quickly come to appreciated how much the mutual suspicion between nurses and doctors got in the way of resolving issues. He smiled at Carlos, thanked him for coming into his office, and explained that he had to prepare for an upcoming meeting. He breathed a sigh of relief after Carlos left.

Later that afternoon, Helen Jung, the head of nursing, came into Graham's office. "Vicki seems to be settling down now," Helen said. "She must have had a good talk with you."

"Good. I tried to listen to her and see her side," Graham said. "I'm convinced that it was a honest mistake that anyone could make."

"Those doctors sure can be high and mighty, always thinking they're right. You'd think Vicki committed a crime! Yet if we ask them to help out when little girls are screaming, they complain and moan that the nurses are insecure. You can't win with these docs."

Graham was sympathetic and let her ventilate. Hadn't he learned at the workshop that leaders listen and show concern for their employees? Yet as she talked, he couldn't help thinking he was becoming a highly paid flak-catcher. Carlos griped about nurses; Helen wailed about doctors. How come we didn't learn more about putting up with angry, self-righteous people in our leadership workshop, Graham wondered, laughing to himself.

Graham decided to get Helen back on an even keel. "The doctors are very concerned about standards, as we all are," he said mildly. "I agree that some of these doctors go overboard, but really we have a lot in common, and there's not that much real conflict."

Graham thought he saw Helen relax somewhat by the time she left. He congratulated himself that he had helped to contain the problem and get people off it. Incidents such as this could be talked about for days and days and really distract people from their work. Rather than focus on how to treat patients, people would gossip and revisit old wounds between nurses and doctors. These distractions then showed up on the "bottom line," as they interfered with productivity, undermined employee commitment to high-quality care, and made Graham's and other administrators' jobs more stressful.

Two days later, Graham was looking forward to his lunch meeting with Maureen and Serge that, at the urging of Richard, they had scheduled while they were at the workshop. He smiled to himself. One good thing about the Vicki incident, he thought, is that I'll have something interesting to talk with them about. Maureen said there's always a good side to a problem.

Maureen, Serge, and Graham enjoyed a spirited, good-natured conversation during lunch. They were still new friends, yet the workshop had demonstrated how much they had in common. After some hesitation, Graham filled them in on the Vicki case. He wanted to let them know more about his situation and to show them how he was putting people leadership to work. As he talked, he realized that they could give him feedback and perspective on the problem.

"Very good," Serge said when Graham was finished. "Sounds like you were both supportive and confrontive with Vicki."

"That's not easy to do," Maureen joined in. "If Vicki had gone back and complained that you didn't listen to her, it would have fed the fire and the nurses would now see you as the enemy. And if you hadn't talked directly to her, the doctors would now see you as the enemy."

"I liked the way that you cooled off the physician and nursing heads," Serge added. "When we have these complaints, I lose my cool too easily and tell people off. I tell them to grow up and quit complaining and just do their job."

"That wouldn't work in a hospital," Graham said.

"It doesn't work at a construction site either," Serge said.

Then Maureen asked a question. "You handled the situation well, Graham, but the underlying problem remains. It's not just that Vicki and Cliff don't communicate and work together well; it's the doctors and nurses who don't. They don't respect each other, they don't trust each other, they don't share resources, and everything becomes win-lose with them. Who would want to work under those conditions?"

"It's called health care," Graham replied. "If you want to work in health care, Maureen, you have to work in such a climate. It's always—well, almost always—like that. I guess you can find some small-town hospitals were doctors and nurses even like each other."

"Ugh. I'll take the sewage business any day," Maureen declared.

"The names and places are different, but we have the same level of mistrust in construction, at least in my company," Serge added. "What can you do?"

"Our boss says her leadership motto is, 'If things aren't hot, then stir the pot,'" Maureen remarked. "She believes in using conflict to get people to deal with their mistrust and bring people together."

"That's wild," Serge exclaimed. "Does that work? She sounds tough!"

"She's tough and soft at the same time," Maureen answered meditatively. "She's upbeat, but if she thinks people are at odds with each other and aren't talking about it, she'll insist that they sit down and get some resolution."

"Interesting, but strange too," Graham mused.

"These confrontations work to give us a good climate," Maureen said. "I appreciated them even more after I heard all those stories at Richard's workshop."

"I think I use the opposite leadership motto: 'When things get hot, *cool* the pot,'" Graham said. "But isn't that leadership? I thought we were supposed to defuse conflict, not feed it. I don't see how stirring the pot nurtures people. People don't like conflict."

"But the situation you have now isn't good either for people or for productivity," Maureen said. "I don't see how the nurses, the doctors, or the clinic wins when they mistrust each other so much. They're not coordinating well. They're not learning much from each other. It will be dry timber ready to burst into flame when another Vicki-type incident happens. Then you'll have to mollify them again and patch things up. You'll feel tired at the end of the week, but whether you'll feel effective at the end of the year is another matter."

Graham wasn't sure he understood everything that Maureen was saying, but he decided it was important for him to consider it. "So what would your boss do in my shoes?"

"I'm not sure. But she might get the nurses and physicians in one room and tell them to talk about their feelings and attitudes toward each other and make some plans for how to improve them. Perhaps it'd make sense to begin with the heads, then work down, since there are so many people involved."

"I don't think I'm ready for that, and I *know* the docs and nurses aren't," Graham said. "They'd laugh at me if I suggested it."

"Let them," Maureen said. "Tell them you're in this job to do something, to make change, not to keep things the same."

"Okay, maybe I can handle that part. But if they're in the same room, who's going to keep it under control? Nasty, hurtful things will be said. People will go too far. I know it."

"Good point," Maureen said. "It may be too extreme, and I agree that you don't want to do something that might get out of control. I'm just trying to stretch our thinking."

"Still, it's a very interesting idea," Serge said. "Thought-provoking. But I'm with Graham. I'm not ready to do it either."

"It seems so simple and so complex at the same time," Graham said. "I agree it would be win-win for everyone if we could do something about people's mistrust. But changing attitudes has always seemed so futile, so impossible."

"But that's just how we can have an impact, really make a difference," Maureen protested. "Just think about how much more productive the clinic would be, how much better it would be for the people working there, if the nurses and doctors really respected each other and worked together!"

"That's a vision, Maureen," Serge said, shaking his head.

"It's a dream," Graham said knowingly.

Focusing on Relationships

The leadership workshop and his discussion with Maureen and Serge focused Graham on the pervasive impact of relationships at the clinic. When he supported and listened to Vicki, he learned more about the causes of the problem and got to know Vicki better. She became less fearful and more committed to the clinic. Instead of spreading hostility, she reassured the other nurses that Graham could understand their perspective.

Graham had long known that there was tension and mistrust between the doctors and nurses, but it was so ingrained and long-standing that it had been easy for him to overlook its impact. Nurses and physicians blamed each other so often that their hostility needed no explanation. Graham assumed it was natural and inevitable, in fact. Doctors were inevitably arrogant, nurses were always insecure and bitter, and hospitals and clinics were tough places to work, period. Professionals and nonprofessionals had prejudices and grievances against each other. That was the way things were and always would be.

But Graham was now realizing that this mistrust distorted the impact of his own actions and weakened his leadership. The other physicians saw Graham's openness and support of Vicki as a hostile, ineffectual action. For them, he was being too soft, too "people-oriented," at the expense of their interests and standards. Graham also saw more clearly that the rancor between physicians and nurses lay at the root of the tetanus shot incident and many of the clinic's other problems.

An incident like the one with Vicki was actually less distracting than the mistrust that underlay people's reactions to it. People would always make mistakes; the issue was whether they would learn from those mistakes or try to blame them on their rivals. Now Maureen was challenging Graham to explore ways to mitigate the hostile relationship between the physicians and nurses.

Graham was also confronting his either-or thinking. He once would have thought that his only options were to support Vicki or to confront her. He was either on the side of the nurses or on the side of the physicians. He would have thought that he could exercise either people leadership or task leadership but not both. He could be good either for people or for productivity.

But Maureen argued that the interests of the physicians, the nurses, and the clinic all went together. Everyone suffered from mistrustful relationships; they would all gain from high-quality relationships. The nurses and physicians would work together and learn from their mistakes; patients would be treated more as valued customers. Graham could lead both physicians and nurses; he could provide both people leadership and task leadership.

Discussing the Vicki incident with Maureen and Serge challenged Graham to reconsider his handling of it. In particular, it brought relationship between nurses and doctors from the background to the foreground. Graham was beginning to take a broad leadership view and to see new possibilities for how he could have a more enduring impact.

The Need for Theory of Relationships

Graham was surprised and intrigued by Maureen's challenge to his basic ideas about the nature of ideal relationships in organizations. He had assumed that productive relationships were relatively free of conflict and that conflicts that did emerge were to be dealt with quickly and expeditiously. This assumption seemed so commonsensical that he had never even questioned it.

Now he saw that this unexamined assumption had very much guided how he handled the tetanus shot incident. He had tried to mollify Vicki, Carlos, and Helen and get them to put the conflict behind them. People at Cedar Lake had congratulated him on his success when he did. What he had failed to do, however, was to use the conflict to deal with the ongoing hostility between the nurses and physicians.

Knowing that his own motives were honest and noble, he had blamed the narrow-mindedness and mean-spiritedness of the physicians and nurses for the problem. But could he himself be part of the problem? Perhaps he had allowed, even made it easy for them to be at odds with each other. He had kept the fire from getting too hot and taken on some of the blame. He had acted as a communication link and intermediary, making it unnecessary for them to try to solve problems together, face to face. He realized these solutions were far from optimal, but he thought that they were the best that could be done.

Breaking away from old assumptions and habits, Graham was getting prepared to experiment with new ways to lead. But he feared taking risks. He needed a reliable model of the kinds of relationships he should strive to achieve, and he needed practical, effective ways of developing them. In Part Two, we will see Graham learning the theory of cooperation and powerful ways to strengthen cooperative relationships.

Leadership as Teamwork

Guides for Action

- Foster trust in the workplace.
- Identify relationship issues that underlie frequent troubles.
- Develop an understanding of the nature of productive relationships.
- Invest in the long-term by building productive relationships.
- Confront either-or thinking.

Pitfalls to Avoid

- Mollifying every conflict to keep the peace.
- Accepting suspicion and mistrust as inevitable in working relationships.
- Letting everyone lose from mistrustful relationships.
- Assuming your beliefs about the nature of productive relationships are true.
- Believing there is an inherent tradeoff between leading for people and leading for productivity.
- Hoping someone else will take the risk of trying to strengthen relationships.

PART TWO

Understanding Relationships
Cooperation and Competition Theory

There is no hope for creating a better world without a deeper scientific insight in the function of leadership and culture, and of other essentials of group life.
—*Kurt Lewin, early social psychologist*

Leaders can have a long-term impact on people and productivity by using cooperation theory to develop effective relationships throughout an organization. To realize this potential, leaders must shed whatever outworn notions they may have about cooperation and conflict. Research has documented that sharing cooperative goals helps people and groups to integrate their ideas and energy and to use conflict so that they are empowered to serve customers and innovate. The essence of cooperation is for people to support each other to achieve mutual goals. It can be implemented in many different ways.

Leaders begin with themselves and develop a cooperative team that will reflect and strengthen their leadership abilities. They seek the feedback and emotional support of their colleagues, employees, and other partners because learning and applying cooperation theory requires creative problem solving and courageous risk taking. Leaders must be savvy if they are to develop a strong cooperative culture in which people are convinced that they are all on the same side.

5

The Cooperative Leader

The reason we were so good, and continued to be so good, was because [Joe Paterno] forces you to develop an inner love among the players. It is much harder to give up on your buddy than it is to give up on your coach. I really believe that over the years the teams I played on were almost unbeatable in tight situations. When we needed to get that six inches we got it because of our love for each other. Our camaraderie existed because of the kind of coach and the kind of person Joe was.
—Dave Joyner, former Penn Sate football player

"Carlos told me right in this office that the doctors are concerned about their relationship with the nurses," Graham told a disbelieving Helen. Graham had gathered the courage to ask Carlos if he thought there was a problem in the relationship between physicians and nurses, and he had been surprised and relieved when Carlos had unequivocally agreed there was. "He said there should be more cooperation," Graham repeated to Helen.

"I believe that," Helen replied. "Those docs are always talking about cooperation and then having us shut up and do what we're told. They like cooperation—as long as it means us cooperating with their terms."

Graham was taken aback, unsure what to say. The gap between the ideal and the actual relationship between physicians and nurses was so large, so encumbered by so much history, that it might be impossible to close it. "I think we have to be willing to start fresh," he ventured tentatively.

"You expect me to tell my nurses to forgive and forget? We have good reason not to trust the physicians! Get all new doctors, and give them some training. Then I'll tell the nurses we'll make a fresh start. We know these doctors."

Graham didn't like Helen's perspective, but he wasn't sure how to rebut her. Although he himself was a physician, he understood that the nurses had legitimate grievances and that his suggestion to forgive and forget might not be very realistic. "It seems a shame to go on and on like this, both sides mistrusting the other," Graham lamented.

"Of course it is. It's a waste." Helen stopped for a moment to mourn past battles, then quickly said, "We know it's a waste. We're the ones that pay for it."

Before his conversation with Maureen, Graham would have tried to move away from this hot topic, but now he wanted to pursue it. "Guess what?" he said to Helen. "Carlos said something very similar, except he said it's the doctors who pay. I think we all pay. Perhaps we can agree on that?"

"Docs do not *pay*. They *get* paid."

"I don't think I accomplished very much," Graham told Maureen and Serge. They had all decided to meet regularly as a study group to discuss their situations and learn more about leadership. Graham had filled them in on his attempts to get nurses and physicians to focus on their relationship.

"At least you brought up the issue and got them talking about it," Serge said.

"We may not be talking about pushing the limits of managerial courage here, Graham, but it was a useful move," Maureen said. "You can't expect change overnight."

Graham smiled. Serge's and Maureen's comments reaffirmed the encouragement he'd gotten from Nora. "It was an adventure, in a way. Nothing really awful happened. They both saw it as a problem, and both seem interested in talking about it. But doing something would be difficult," he concluded.

"You can see how their attitudes and mistrust get in the way," Serge said. "They each blame the problems on the other side."

"They blame the other side when the tetanus shot isn't given. They blame the other side because they can't work together," Maureen commented.

"A vicious cycle," Serge put in.

"Sounds like each side sees that it pays a price, but neither is sure that the other side pays," Maureen said.

"Each side believes it wants to work well and improve the relationship, but it doubts the other is willing," Serge agreed.

"So much mistrust," Graham said, sighing.

"They even mistrust what each other says," Maureen observed. "Carlos says he wants to cooperate, and Helen thinks he wants to tell them what to do."

"What a quagmire," Serge exclaimed.

"One thing that we did at our place that helped was to arrive at a common understanding of what we meant by working together," Maureen said. "Then we brainstormed what specific behaviors would help us work cooperatively."

"But Helen does have a point," Graham objected. "It's not realistic to expect the nurses to put their grudges aside just like that, even though we know they should."

"That's the beauty of this theory that we work with," Maureen said. "When people cooperate, then they're *going* to conflict."

"You're playing with words, Maureen," Graham said.

"Not really," Maureen said. "It's a very important point: People who work together are still going to disagree about many, many things. They're going to disagree about how to get the job done and about who should do what task."

"And about who gets what reward," Serge added.

"There are so many issues that it's not realistic to expect that they're always going to agree," Maureen said.

"That's interesting." Graham didn't want to appear defensive to Maureen and Serge. "But I thought that when people are cooperative, they work harmoniously, without conflict."

"People can want the same thing and be united in their goal but still disagree over how to get there," Maureen explained. "You and your boss both want to improve the clinic, right? But he wants to spend money on technology, while you want to spend money on nurturing people."

"I think Maureen is saying, don't confuse working cooperatively with never disagreeing," Serge said. "Helen could buy into this way of thinking."

"But it's not going to work to let Helen and the nurses rip into the doctors," Graham protested. "I know I'm not *that* courageous!"

"Of course not—you don't want people just letting it all hang out and complaining about everyone," Maureen said. "But when people disagree yet remember that they're still working together and aren't trying to win, then they're able to deal with their conflicts well."

Graham wanted to follow Maureen's reasoning, but he felt overwhelmed. "I hope you have something I could read about this."

"I've a book and an article or two I could let you have," Maureen assured him.

"Thanks," Graham said. "It seems to me that when people are in a fight, what they're trying to do is win. Who would want to lose?"

"But both people can win—at least, both people can benefit from a good resolution of a conflict," Maureen said.

"Don't they call that win-win negotiating?" Serge asked.

"You mean that they end up with some sort of compromise," Graham said. "But doesn't that just dilute things, so they end up with muddled answers?"

"Groupthink sort of thing," Serge clarified.

"Sometimes a compromise is what you want," Maureen replied. "But often a good discussion of differences doesn't result in a muddling compromise but in a much better, clearer decision that leaves everyone better off."

"Designing a house can be that way," Serge said thoughtfully. "I've been in big fights with some architects, but in the end we built a tastefully designed house that wasn't too costly."

"I suppose you all are going to tell me next that conflict is a good thing," Graham said.

"It can be a bad thing, it can be an okay thing, and it can be a terrific thing," Maureen said. "It depends on whether you are cooperating effectively."

"This is going to be hard," Graham mused. "We have a lot of pretty big egos in the clinic, and they all want things their way."

"They're like the rest of us," Serge said. "They have to learn that they can't always have things their way."

"Agreed," Maureen said. "But when you work cooperatively, you don't have to give up your goals and interests either. We're not talking about altruism here."

"But how are they supposed to work cooperatively and work for themselves too?" Graham argued.

"In cooperation, you work for yourself *and* for others. Everyone wants to achieve," Maureen said.

"They help each other get where they want to go," Serge said.

"That's a good way of putting it," Maureen said.

"I have lots to read and think about," Graham said.

Getting Focused on Theory

Graham had analyzed the mistrust between the nurses and the physicians as a problem in motivation and as a history of conflict. He decided they were angry with each other and uninterested in developing their relationship. But he was now beginning to appreciate that unclear ideas also contributed to the problem. When the physicians argued for more cooperation, the nurses assumed that the physicians wanted them to acquiesce. Feeling slighted and irritated that the nurses would not respond to a reasonable request, the physicians for their part concluded that the nurses were mean-spirited and unwilling to cooperate.

Graham had his confusions too. He recognized the inadequacy of his assumption that productive relationships are conflict-free, but he was unsure how cooperation relates to altruism and conflict. Maureen and Serge argued that cooperation doesn't mean the same thing as harmony or selflessness. People who work cooperatively pursue their interests as they promote the goals of others. They debate and fight over many issues and ideas. What direction they should take, the means they employ to achieve their goal, the division of work, and the distribution of rewards—all these are major points of contention.

Effectively discussed conflict has proved to be a useful complement to cooperative goals. Effective negotiation irons out difficulties and invigorates; lively debate makes cooperative work more vibrant and productive. A clear understanding of cooperation and conflict would help Graham lead the Cedar Lake Clinic from mistrust to productive relationships.

Cooperation and Competition

In the 1940s, Morton Deutsch, a pioneering social psychologist from Columbia University, proposed that how people believe their goals are related determines their expectations, interactions, and effectiveness. Hundreds of studies have subsequently developed this theory and shown it to be an elegant, powerful way to understand joint effort and conflict.

Different interactions can have very different characteristics. People's beliefs about how they depend upon each other drastically affect their expectations, communication, exchange, problem solving, and productivity. Deutsch theorized that whether people believe their goals are predominantly cooperative or competitive will affect their expectations and actions and thereby the consequences of interaction.

The Alternatives

People working cooperation believe that their goals are positively related, so that as one person moves toward her goal, all move toward reaching their goal. They understand that as one person succeeds, others succeed. People in cooperation want each other to pursue their goal effectively, since one's effectiveness helps all of them reach their goal. If one swims, the other swims; if one sinks, the other sinks. They feel like a team.

The achievement of each individual depends upon the achievements of the others. Cooperation is based not on altruism but on the recognition that, with positively related goals, self-interest requires collaboration. Team members who are responsible for new product development, for instance, will cooperate to develop useful ideas and work hard to create a new product that makes everyone feel successful. *Cooperative work integrates individual self-interest to achieve compatible goals.*

When people are working against each other, they may believe that their goals are competitive, so that one person's attainment of their goal precludes or at least makes less likely the goal attainment of others. If one person succeeds, others must fail. If one wins, the others must lose. People who are in competition with each other conclude that they are better off when others act ineffectively and that when other people are productive, they themselves are less likely to be successful. Competitive team members want to prove they are the most capable and that their ideas are superior; they are frustrated when others develop useful ideas and

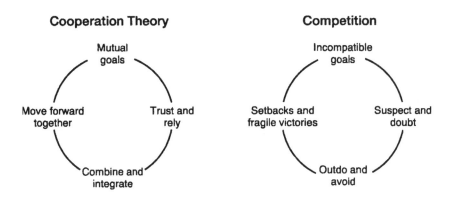

Cooperation Theory	Competition
Mutual goals	Incompatible goals
Move forward together	Setbacks and fragile victories
Trust and rely	Suspect and doubt
Combine and integrate	Outdo and avoid

work hard. *Competitive work pits individual self-interest against one another in a struggle to win.*

Major Propositions

Whether people's goals are primarily cooperative or competitive, Deutsch theorized, profoundly affects their orientation and intentions toward each other. In cooperation, people want others to act effectively, and they expect others to want them to be effective because it is in each person's self-interest to do so. They trust that their efforts will be welcomed and reciprocated. They believe they can rely upon each other, and they are sensitive and responsive to each other.

This mutual expectation of trust leads to discussions of shared perspectives and interests. Studies document that people in cooperation share information, acknowledge each other's perspective, communicate and influence effectively, exchange resources, assist and support each other, discuss opposing ideas openly, and use higher-quality reasoning. These actions, in turn, help cooperators move forward by completing tasks, agreeing to high-quality solutions, reducing stress, fostering attraction, and strengthening work relationships and confidence in future collaboration.

Competitive expectations, on the other hand, lead people to promote their own interests at the expense of others' and even to actively interfere with each other. An atmosphere of mistrust restricts information and resource exchange and distorts communication. People often try to avoid direct discussions, and when compelled to discuss, they impose their positions on each other. These ways of interacting frustrate productivity, intensify stress, and lower morale.

People with cooperative goals can still be in conflict. The word *conflict*, as used here, refers to incompatible activities, in which one person is disagreeing, obstructing, or frustrating another. Cooperative goals promote productive conflict management. With cooperative goals, people freely speak their minds, reveal their frustrations, and talk about their anger. People are open to confrontations and realize it is important to work out settlements so that they can continue to assist each other. They work for mutually beneficial solutions that maintain and strengthen the relationship. They explore each other's perspectives, creatively integrate their views, and are confident they can work together for their mutual benefit. As a result, they are prepared to handle future conflicts.

Competitive goals, by contrast, make managing conflict very difficult and can lead to debilitating fights. With competitive goals, people suspect that pursuing self-interest inevitably leads to mutual frustration. They doubt that other people are interested in their feelings and frustrations, and they fear ridicule. Although they often prefer to avoid conflict, especially with their bosses and others with authority and power who can "win" and impose their wishes, the underlying problems continue to frustrate. If they do decide to confront an antagonist, they often do so in a tough, dominating manner that escalates the conflict. Whether they choose to avoid or to confront conflict, however, competitors usually end up feeling that they have lost, and they can only hope that others have lost more.

Research on Organizational Effectiveness

Recent studies have extended research on the fundamental dynamics and outcomes of cooperation and competition to show how cooperative goals, followed by open discussion and constructive conflict, contribute to organizational effectiveness. For instance, cooperative goals and constructive controversy are critical for serving customers and innovating.

Serving Customers

Contemporary managers recognize that they must stay in touch and listen to their customers. Not only are retail stores and other consumer companies taking their customers more seriously, but professional organizations, governmental agencies, and regulated companies are too. They know they must listen to customers who are frustrated with their service. But listening is only the first step. Companies must also respond to customer complaints and concerns. A successful company is one that listens open-mindedly, acts appropriately, and uses customer problems to improve service and win more customers.

But coordinated action is needed to respond to customer problems successfully. Seldom can the employee who hears a complaint solve the problem alone. The employee who listens must communicate the problem to others and get them to assist in its resolution. Especially in larger, bureaucratic companies, employees from different departments and outlooks have to collaborate.

To demonstrate the value of cooperative work in responding to customers, we interviewed forty-three employees from the customer service division of a large telecommunications company on how they interacted with people from other departments as they dealt with customer problems. We found that employees who had cooperative goals were able to solve customer complaints more successfully than employees with competitive or independent goals. When employees from different departments cooperated, the customers were well served, the company's image was enhanced, time and materials were used efficiently, and employees felt more confident about themselves and their work relationships. In contrast, competitive interactions wasted time and materials, damaged the company's reputation, and undermined future work.

Cooperative work is also necessary for identifying client needs and providing them with valued products and services. Engineering and other consulting companies know that their clients want viable, cost-effective solutions to their problems. Because clients want such solutions, not simply technical expertise, it is not enough to give a client various kinds of engineering knowledge or provide a solution that makes sense from only one standpoint. Clients want a solution that will integrate specialized knowledge into a coherent approach that will work for them. To win and fulfill contracts, engineers within a firm must bring their various areas of expertise and experience to bear and find ways to incorporate them in the solution. Their managers must work to develop a culture, a compensation system, and procedures that encourage and reward such teamwork across specialities.

In one large engineering consulting company, the vice-presidents and executives who manage business development, finance, information systems, project management, pulp and paper, steam and power, civil and structure, mechanical engineering, and fifteen other departments were interviewed on specific times they had worked with managers from other departments. The finding was that engineers who had cooperative but not competitive goals won contracts and improved productivity by using their resources, information, and time wisely. They felt more competent and more confident that they would be able to work together in the future. When they worked competitively, they lost contracts and weakened the company's reputation in the marketplace, wasted time and materials, lowered productivity, and made future productive collaboration less likely. These consequences cost the company money and hurt its bottom line.

Salespeople often rely upon a network of people within their organization to serve customers. They turn to managers and specialists to help them structure specific price and service agreements and to facilitate their effective implementation. Thirty salespersons with an average of ten years of experience working for a large industrial supplier with a client base in lumber, pulp, and mining were interviewed about specific times they had worked with others in their company to try to serve customers. Salespersons who believed their goals were cooperative rather than competitive with other members of their organization discussed issues thoroughly and developed plans productive for themselves, the organization, and customers. With these dynamics and strong relationships, the salespersons were motivated to serve customers, and they learned how to improve their service in the future. Cooperative interactions also facilitated their completing tasks, efficiency, confidence in future collaboration, and positive feelings. Research has documented the value of cooperative goals in fostering the collaboration needed between salespersons and others in the company to serve customers.

Customers are not served by the skill and flair of an individual salesperson. To market high technology effectively, for example, service, training, engineering, and technical personnel must coordinate with each other and with salespersons. Cooperative goals promote the open, lively discussions that result in integrated, creative solutions that solve problems and create value for customers.

Cooperative goals and positive conflict management also contribute to developing constructive relationships with customers. In high-quality relationships, salespersons are helpful to customers both before and after a sale; they disclose themselves as people, and they indicate they want to maintain a relationship that leads to repeat business in the future. A recent study documents the value of cooperative teamwork in working with customers. Twenty-five salespersons of a large international airline and forty travel agents and managers in charge of corporate travel described specific interactions. When the sales representatives and their customers believed their goals were cooperatively related, they trusted that they could rely on each other, felt accepted, and avoided trying to dominate. They went out of their way to assist each other, give information, and explain issues. They explored their different views to solve problems and used their conflicts to strengthen their relationships.

In cooperation, salespersons and clients felt good about their interaction, made progress solving the problem and getting the task accomplished, worked efficiently, formed a stronger work relationship, and had confidence they could work successfully in the future. Cooperative interactions enhanced sales and reputations.

In contrast, salespersons and clients that had competitive and independent goals tended to be suspicious, avoided open and constructive discussions of ideas and differences, and attempted to dominate each other; they had negative feelings, failed to make much progress on their tasks, worked inefficiently, weakened their relationships, and had doubts about future collaboration. They refused to listen and accommodate, lost sales, and felt disappointed and embarrassed.

Research supports the argument that cooperative relationships with customers are critical because they bind customers to the company, provide useful information on the company's products and services, and lead to reliable repeat business. When sales representatives and customers develop strongly cooperative goals, they manage conflict, solve problems, and form positive expectations of future encounters.

Cooperative goals build the spirited teamwork necessary for people within a company to serve each other. Then the company can consistently deliver high-quality products and services and respond to customer complaints effectively. Cooperation and skillful conflict are also critical for external service to help salespeople and other company representatives reach out and establish continuing relationships with customers.

Innovation

Organizations that do not serve their customers wither. But organizations must also innovate, so that they will be prepared to serve customers in the future with quality products at competitive prices. Diversity in the workforce and the new sensitivity to sexual harrassment and other issues also require management changes. While organizations are experimenting with new procedures and management styles, they are developing new products and services to respond to changes in technology, competition, and consumer preferences.

In one study, faculty members and employees of a large postsecondary educational institution were interviewed about when they were able to solve problems in new and creative ways, and when they were frustrated, unable to develop a new approach. When they discussed their opposing views openly and forthrightly and considered all views, they were able to develop innovative solutions. When they discussed issues competitively, from only one point of view, and were unable to incorporate different views, they failed to make progress and developed solutions low in quality and creativity.

Managers have long complained that employees resist new technological innovations and that, as a consequence, investments do not pay off in the expected productivity increases. What is less recognized is that employees must identify problems and discuss solutions to use the technology. Cooperative employees of a retail chain, for example, were able to use new scanning technology efficiently because they exchanged information and hammered out ideas about how to solve the many problems the technology created.

Managers are restructuring and transforming organizations today. They are cutting management levels, splitting up businesses, forming links across business units, and using task teams and parallel structures to create synergy. However, restructuring seldom results in the expected improved quality of products, productivity, and quality of work life for employees and returns for shareholders. A large high-technology telecommunications firm underwent waves of restructuring, without noticeable improvement. Interviews revealed that changing the structures alone had been insufficient. The employees had to make use of the new structures, and to do this, they had to coordinate and manage their conflicts. When their goals were cooperative, they were able to manage their difficulties and reassure and support each other so that they could make use of the new structures.

Many companies rely on performance appraisal systems to promote employee development. But the utility of performance appraisal depends in large part on the effective discussion of opposing views on the employee's performance and plans for improvement. Managers with bosses who dealt with conflicts cooperatively rather than competitively or avoided them rated the quality of the feedback high, felt more motivated to work hard, were more committed to the performance appraisal, and were confident they could work well with their boss in the future.

Graham, struggling to understand the importance of cooperative relationships for leading Cedar Lake, found it intellectually challenging to see the links between cooperative work, conflict, and organizational effectiveness. He also felt the challenge of learning how to apply these ideas. The nurses and physicians kept their distance from each other except in periodic, brief flareups. If they were really to work together, they would have to shed their old ideas and habits in order to trust, communicate openly, and manage conflict constructively. Graham knew it would not be easy, but a validated theory of productive relationships could be extremely useful. As we will see in the next chapter, Graham would begin to apply cooperation theory to his leadership.

Cooperative Leadership

Guides for Action

- Use cooperation theory to clarify confusions about nature of productive relationships.
- Identify instances of cooperation, competition, and conflict in your organization.
- Establish cooperative goals that will empower people to serve customers well and to innovate.

Pitfalls to Avoid

- Adhering closedmindedly to your notions of productive relationships.
- Assuming that cooperation implies harmonious uniformity.
- Believing that cooperation requires altruism.
- Equating conflict with competition.

6

Building on Cooperation Theory

If we have no sense of community, the American dream will continue to wither. Our destiny is bound up with the destiny of every American. We're all in this together, and we will rise or fall together. . . . Together we can do it. Together we can make the country that we love everything it was meant to be.

—*U.S. President Bill Clinton*

Graham decided to get Carlos, Helen, and Louis Kirby, the head of housekeeping and maintenance, more involved in making major equipment-purchasing decisions. Perhaps, if they made purchases together, they would make better decisions and would share the new equipment more efficiently. There might be fewer questions and criticisms later. It would be a good example, Graham thought of people leadership at work.

His conversations with Maureen and Serge about cooperation and conflict had helped him feel more relaxed about the doctor-nurse hostility. Telling Carlos and Helen that he was committed to making the best decisions for the whole clinic and that he wanted to hear their opinions had a positive, if modest impact, he thought.

"It was a good discussion," Carlos told Graham later. "But you seem like you are against buying my new machine."

"We have to look very closely at new technology that costs real money. Our budget situation is probably going to get worse." Graham paused, then continued. "I have another question. Some time ago, we talked about getting more cooperation between nurses and doctors here. Do you still want to do something?"

"Sure. It's needed here,—probably more than in most places."

"What do you think this cooperation would look like?"

"People pulling together, I guess. Remembering our common goals and not getting hung up on our differences."

Graham wanted to encourage Carlos. "I'm glad you're interested," he said.

"Of course, cooperation has limits too. We have too much work to do to get everyone together all the time. As I've always argued, doctors have to be able to make the medical decisions. It would be irresponsible for us to let others do it. Cooperation, like anything else, can be overdone."

"Seems reasonable." Graham thought this fit the contingency theories he learned about at the workshop: There is no one leadership approach appropriate for all situations, and leaders must act in ways that fit the circumstances.

"It would be wrong to suppress the individual too much," Carlos added. "It's still the individual that makes this place go around. Each person has to do his job well, or we're not a good clinic."

"Individuals have to have responsibility, and they must be held accountable," Graham agreed. "People are always ready to escape responsibility by blaming the group. 'It was the group's decision, I didn't do it.'"

"We can't stop in the middle of an operation to get everyone's ideas about how to proceed." Carlos laughed.

"We're not crazy." Enjoying himself, Graham wondered why he and Carlos hadn't had discussions like this before now.

"We also need competition around here to give us a shot," Carlos continued. "I think our critics have a point. We do need competition, a market approach to give us more drive toward efficiency. In a way, we've been too cooperative, too lax."

"Interesting."

Carlos, too, relished an intellectual discussion about something besides medicine. "Cooperation is fine. But you've got to keep things in perspective. You can't go overboard. Sometimes people have to be autocratic; you can't always be democratic and participatory. Sometimes you have to be decisive and take a stand."

Two days before the next study group meeting, Graham telephoned Maureen and Serge and told them about Carlos's argument that organizations need competition as well as cooperation. They promised to study their books and articles to prepare for a good discussion.

When they met two days later, they talked over recent events, then Graham summarized his discussion with Carlos. "So it's not simply cooperation that we have to foster," he concluded, "but also competition and independent work."

"It gets difficult and confusing fast, unfortunately," Serge remarked.

"In the abstract, I think his argument is quite reasonable," Maureen said. "But the practical issue is still how to increase the cooperation between the nurses and doctors. At Cedar Lake, you don't need more people doing their own thing or competing against each other, Graham, do you?"

"Not really, but we still need to know how competition and working by yourself fit in," Graham said. "These medical people are a hard-nosed lot, very research-oriented. They'll ask lots of questions, and they'll be skeptical about general solutions. Carlos won't be the only one to talk about the limits to cooperation. I'll have to have an answer for them."

"I read an article that described cooperation as the basis, with people working as individuals within it," Maureen said slowly. "The group assigns people work, then holds them accountable. So they're working independently and as part of a group, both at the same time."

"So individuals are still held accountable in cooperation," Graham said.

"Accountability to the group could be very strong," Serge said. "I know my people don't want to displease their peers, even less than they want to displease their boss. The customer is farther down the list."

"I suppose you're going to tell me you compete and cooperate at the same time." Graham laughed.

"You can," Maureen answered. "The article gave the example of departments competing over which could raise the most money for a charity. Yet their real goal was to raise money and build their team spirit."

"It's like when you bet playing golf. You want to win, but the most important thing is to enjoy a round of golf with your friends," Serge said. "Or you'll soon have to find new golf partners."

"But you need competition within yourself to strive to do your best, to do a quality job," Graham said.

"Cooperation needs a commitment to doing a job well too. That's why everyone has to pitch together," Maureen said. "Having people compete against each other isn't going to help an organization do quality jobs."

"But Carlos has a point," Graham argued. "We can't always discuss and do things as a group. Democracy isn't always the best way of operating. Sometimes you have to take a stand."

"But cooperation doesn't mean that people do everything as a group or always operate as a democracy," Maureen said. "Cooperation has to do with attitudes and feelings about each other, not with procedures and strategies."

"How can you be cooperative and autocratic at the same time?" Serge asked.

"It's not realistic to get everyone involved in making all decisions," Maureen replied, "but people can still feel that they are all in it together. There are some people who are seldom involved in making decisions but who still feel cooperative toward management."

"But other people are always involved and *never* feel cooperative," Serge said.

"It works both ways," Maureen agreed.

"But you can't talk about cooperation and then go ahead and make all the decisions yourself," Graham said.

"I think you're right," Maureen said. "In cooperation, everyone is important. If you never solicit their ideas and suggestions, then people might not believe that you think they're important. So there's overlap. But operating cooperatively doesn't mean that you're always democratic and always have a consensus."

"So I don't always have to be democratic. That's good." Still, Graham had a more fundamental objection. "Is everyone equal in cooperation, Maureen? That would be very difficult sell in a clinic."

"Not everyone is identical, but everyone is equal in that they are a person and do valuable tasks," Maureen said.

"Including the janitors?" Graham asked.

"You want to work in a messy clinic? You hire people and pay them money because a job needs to be done, right?" Maureen said.

"But some people and some jobs are more important than others," Graham said. "You can't pay everyone the same, Maureen."

"In our market economy, giving everyone the same pay isn't very realistic. But respecting everyone is," Maureen said. "Everyone is part of the team. Everyone contributes. Everyone counts. Emphasizing that some people are more important than others only gets you in trouble."

"So I don't have to sell my managers on the idea that every decision must be made by a group, but I do have to convince them that everyone is important." Graham paused. "That might be even harder," he said.

"Working cooperatively sounds simple, but it seems that seldom is," Serge commented.

Graham had more than enough to think about now. The conclusions he and Carlos had reached about a contingency approach to cooperation and the need to balance cooperation with competition and independence had seemed so sensible, but now he saw their limitations. "I appreciate the help from both of you. This must be a little boring for you, Maureen, because you've been over these ideas before," Graham said.

"I'm happy to do it," Maureen said. "But really, it's more challenging than boring. Rereading and discussing cooperation helps me put things in words. It's so vast an idea, and we have so many stereotypes that I need to read and discuss it several times. One speaker we heard said she had been studying it for twenty years, and she kept learning more about cooperation."

"One of the main ideas I got out of this,"—Graham worked to summarize his thoughts—"is that cooperation is the core of productive relationships. This means that we often do things in groups and operate in a consensus, but not always."

"One last thing," Maureen said. "You have to let Carlos know that in cooperation people certainly do take a stand. They mix it up, even push each other to change."

"Cooperation is not a rose garden," Serge said.

The Forms of Cooperation

Carlos's and Graham's assumptions interfered with their understanding of cooperation. They both assumed that cooperation was a particular style of behaving and organizing: Groups were structured, leaders were participatory, and people were gentle with each other. But through his discussion with Maureen and Serge, Graham distinguished between the form and essence of cooperation, between the procedures and the core of cooperation.

The essence of cooperation is people supporting each other and working together to pursue their mutual goals. But cooperation takes many forms beyond that essence. Instituting a task force or new product team does not necessarily mean the team members will work cooperatively. They may not feel they are in it together, or they may not even be interested in promoting each other's goals. They may believe that they should use the task force only to defend their department's interests. Having a leader who tries to be participatory by asking for input does not automatically make people believe that furthering management's interests further theirs. They may even think that participation is a trap to coopt them and frustrate their aspirations.

Cooperative interaction is much richer and more complex than Carlos, Graham, and many others assume. A common confusion is to assume that cooperation means that people are "kind" and "gentle" and must suppress their assertiveness and their individuality. But as we have seen, conflict is part of cooperation. In cooperation, people actually feel more confident about speaking their minds and expressing their opinions.

Cooperation promotes individual and team accountability and responsibility. Individuals have their own tasks, and they see how these tasks fit in with those of others; they are held accountable by their peers as well as by their supervisors. Teams are held accountable by other teams and by executives. Paradoxically, effective cooperation requires and fosters individuality and diversity.

Nor does working cooperatively mean leaving common sense behind. Some issues are simply not important, complex, or controversial enough to warrant a group discussion. Twenty-five-cent problems do not deserve a thousand-dollar process to solve. There are times when practical restraints make joint consideration of problems impractical. Crises may demand immediate, unilateral action. But research shows that cooperative goals and controversy have been critical in helping flight crew members, for example, deal with emergencies.

Most people recognize that organizations and teams must be flexible, and they appreciate it when their time and the organization's resources are used wisely. In organizations with a cooperative framework, people understand when a decision is made without them because of its costs or inconvenience, not because their ideas and interests are not valued.

More generally, individuals, groups, and organizations must develop forms of cooperation that fit their own circumstances, goals, values, structure, culture, and personalities. Some teams need to meet five minutes every day; others, once a month. Not every group needs to meet at seven o'clock Monday morning, but some do. Some sessions require a set agenda; others are more effective when they are free-floating. Procedures to improve team problem solving, such as assigning two subgroups opposing opinions, must be modified to fit the particular situation.

Employees themselves can create cooperative procedures that are appropriate and useful to them. With a good understanding of cooperation, they can brainstorm and decide how to best exchange ideas and resources. They want procedures that will have them work together efficiently and effectively but that will also help them feel supported and valued as unique persons. They can use the issue of developing procedures to work together to increase their feelings that they are in this together. They can develop meeting times, agendas, discussion norms, and other procedures that will help everyone be successful.

Developing a Cooperative Culture

In effective teams and organizations, cooperation is the underlying way that people work. They have a cooperative culture that signals to everyone that they are in this together and that they help each other accomplish their goals. This cooperative culture can be very productive and useful. As we have seen, though, cooperation takes many forms, and competition and independence also play roles as well.

A cooperative culture does not preclude competition and independence. People work independently as part of a cooperative team. Some issues and problems are more efficiently handled by one person working alone. Competition adds variety and spice; two teams compete to make the best suggestion to improve safety, for example. Some competition is inevitable, as when two people compete for the same job. But they always keep sight of the cooperative climate in which they compete. They share the cooperative goal of having a "fair, clean" competition, in which they present themselves as well as possible. Rather than criticize each other, they retain their relationship so that they can work effectively after one of them is promoted. They also continue to work on joint projects.

The essence of a cooperative culture is a mutual commitment to each other and to pursuing each other's interests. But a cooperative culture is developed only with hard work and continual nurturing. People in teams and organizations often get distracted and slip into competition and independence. They may believe that they cannot trust people to help them, that others do not work in the same superior way they do, or that it is easier for them to focus only on their own goals and tasks.

How can leaders work with employees to develop the belief that they share very strong cooperative goals? How can leaders develop a cooperative culture in which competition and independence play their complementary roles?

Group Goals

Leaders must help formulate group goals to engender cooperation. Once a common goal is identified—for instance, making a set of recommendations, developing and producing a new product, or solving a problem—team members must integrate their ideas and develop one solution. Each person signs off on the team's output, indicating that she has contributed to and supports it. All workers average their individual output to form a group average for each week.

Leaders can emphasize learning as an important cooperative goal. Each worker is responsible for keeping his own output up and for helping others improve theirs. All group members are expected to improve their professional skills.

Group Rewards

Leaders can also use group rewards to help team members understand that their own individual reward depends upon the team's progress. If the team is successful, they will receive both tangible and intangible benefits. Either everyone on the team is rewarded, or no one is rewarded. The team's accomplishments can be recognized in the company newsletter or honored with a party. Each team member receives a monetary bonus based on the team's success, say, five percent of the profits for a new product that the team developed and manufactured.

In many cases, unequal rewards produce rivalry over who should get the larger benefit. But unequal rewards can be effective if people agree that an unequal division is justified. If the task force leader is given five percent of the cost savings from the first year's use of a new inventory system, each member may accept three percent as reasonable because the task force leader was required to do much more work.

Cooperation does not imply that everyone is rewarded or that no one is ever punished. Public humiliation is seldom useful, but managers do need to confront unproductive teams. If a team is unsuccessful, its members will suffer the consequences. The leader confronts poor quality and takes appropriate action, such as noting the group failure in the members' performance appraisal reviews. Managers avoid the temptation to blame a few, but they hold the group as a whole responsible.

Of course, at times an individual, through either a lack of motivation or ability, will frustrate group progress. A leader expects that team members will deal with such individuals early, not wait until the group has failed and then blame the person for their failure. With or without the leader, team members decide how to help the unproductive individual understand the value of his work, train him in needed skills, or replace him.

Connected Roles

Leaders show team members how their complementary, interconnected roles foster cooperation. Each team member has a role
that needs to be performed if the team is to function properly. To
package fresh fish, for example, one employee wheels the correct
size fish to the processing line, two employees cut and clean
the fish, and another packages it into boxes. Employees recognize that they all must fulfill their role obligations to complete
the task.

At Esteven Brick, a large construction company based in
Alberta, team members take turns assuming different group roles.
One person takes the role of devil's advocate to challenge common
views, while another observes. At the end of the meeting the
observer provides feedback to help the group examine and
improve how people are working together.

Scarce, Complementary Resources

Leaders must remind employees that because each of them has
only a portion of the information, abilities, and resources necessary to accomplish the task, they must all contribute. Team members identify their own individual abilities and talents so that they
appreciate how each can move the group toward goal attainment.

Community and Trust

People cooperate because they share a common identity and feel
they belong to one community. They identify with "the Hewlett-
Packard Way" or "the Merck Way," and they see the company as
theirs.

Leaders ask teams to devise and publicize their own name
and symbol. For example, a quality circle group at Musashi Semi-
conductor Works called themselves the Ten Philosophers
and described their personalities on the bulletin board. Team
members focused on their common characteristics and backgrounds.

Trust is typically based on previous experiences of working
together productively. "Small wins," in which a team successfully

achieves a number of well-defined objectives, develop confidence among the team members. People trust those they know and suspect those who remain unknown.

Leaders want team members to know each other as individuals and to enjoy working together. Leaders talk about themselves as people and listen to the ideas and feelings of team members. They all discuss their feelings and the values they consider important. Small talk about family and interests develops personal, trusting relationships.

People trust others who sincerely express warmth, friendliness, and cooperative intentions. Social gatherings such as sports teams and parties encourage such interaction. Team members begin meetings by declaring that they want to work together.

Leaders also model the way by showing they care for individuals and by responding to their needs, celebrating their personal victories, and supporting them in times of crisis. They demonstrate that a person can commit herself to the team because she is accepted, valued, and supported.

Cooperative cultures foster the spirited exchange and teamwork necessary for organizations to serve their customers, to innovate, and to develop the intense internal commitment that employees need in order to be successful. A cooperative culture underlies a productive, fair company that values and listens to all its employees.

The essence of cooperation is not rigid adherence to democratic or other procedures but people supporting and cheering each other on as they work to pursue their mutual goals. Together they develop task forces, participatory decision making, work teams, and other forums that help them influence each other effectively, value each other's diverse styles and opinions, and combine their energy and insights.

Building on Cooperation Theory

Guides for Action

- Recognize that cooperation fosters individuality.
- Work together to develop cooperative policies, systems, and procedures appropriate for people and their situation.

- Formulate group goals and tasks.
- Make rewards contingent upon team success.
- Show how scarce resources makes cooperation imperative.
- Assign complementary roles.
- Value everyone as a person.
- Praise every job well done for contributing to the organization's success.
- Have people disclose their values, aspirations, and feelings.
- Treat people fairly and as distinct individuals with their own personalities and styles.
- Develop ways to hold teams and individuals accountable.
- Confront teams and people honestly when they don't perform.

Pitfalls to Avoid

- Confusing cooperation with avoiding group or individual accountability.
- Equating cooperation with holding meetings and deciding by majority vote.
- Speaking about the need to cooperate and assign tasks and rewards to individuals.
- Lavishing resources so that individuals believe they can do tasks by themselves.
- Valuing people according to their knowledge, income, or position.
- Trying to treat everyone identically.

7

Learning to Use Cooperation Theory

He that will not apply new remedies must expect new evils: for time is the greatest innovator.

—*Sir Francis Bacon*

"How am I supposed to get turkeys to cooperate?" Graham asked Nora as they took a walk before dinner one evening. "It's not just nurses and doctors who don't get it. Maintenance and housekeeping are just as bad!"

Graham explained that Louis Kirby, the head of housekeeping and maintenance, had complained for over an hour about being understaffed.

"Maybe he really needs more people," Nora suggested.

"That's not so simple—especially with our budget getting tighter. No, Louis was venting his anger. He railed against the nurses and physicians for making ugly, unnecessary messes and never picking up after themselves, for demanding quick repair and service even if they're over budget, and on and on. What was really bothering him was that he and his group don't feel respected."

"Did he say that?"

"No, but you don't have to be an expert in body language to read between the lines when Louis talks."

"Another leadership challenge." Nora considered Graham's talking about this problem so directly with her as progress.

"Right." Graham himself was giving vent to frustrations and discouragement. "All those speeches by politicians and other so-called leaders about what we can do if we join forces, if we have a common vision, if we are united and work together—they make it sound so easy."

Nora laughed. "They talk about it as if talking would make it happen."

"But talk doesn't."

"People know that too. People normally talk about things that haven't happened, that aren't easy to do. If people were united, then why would they go on and on about it? If it were easy to do, it would have been done already."

"You've got a point." Graham was grateful that talking with Nora relieved some of his discouragement. But he soon focused on the obstacles he faced. "I've been talking and reading about cooperation and getting so I understand it, but now what do I do with it?"

Nora didn't want to make her Rome-wasn't-built-in-a-day speech again. "You're making progress—that's what's important," she said instead.

"When I told Louis that we needed more cooperation among the different groups, he agreed, then went right on complaining. It's not as if people shrug the idea off or disagree, but they just keep doing the same thing they were doing before. Who can disagree with cooperation, at least in the abstract?"

"It's doing it that's the rub. It's hard for people to change."

"It's hard even for me to change. I'm learning some new ideas, but I don't know how to implement them at the clinic. Just telling people they should cooperate doesn't do it."

"Yes, that would get old fast."

"They'd tune me out, even get mad at me for badgering them about working together."

"You'd sound like a politician. You've got to be credible. So you have to *act* cooperatively as well as *talk* about it. People have heard so many nice-sounding words from the top of the organization, with so little effect on how the company actually works. Have Maureen and Serge given you any suggestions?"

"Maureen said her whole group met for three days offsite about how they could become a cooperative team organization. Everyone got involved and worked on how the whole group could become more cooperative and effective."

"That's exciting. I can see a big payoff in that."

"But it's totally impractical for us. Our people just aren't ready for it. I can hear the screaming already—'How can we shut down the clinic and spend three days discussing relationships!' Even if we did get together, who knows what craziness would happen? It's too risky. My boss won't support it. It's a nonstarter."

"But you could get someone from outside to facilitate a workshop and keep it under control."

"Who would hang around to do that after the workshop was over?" Graham paused. "Even more to the point, *I'm* not ready. I don't think I could answer the skeptics' questions. I'm certainly not confident I could manage a workshop."

"Why not live dangerously?"

"Nora, I've been trained to be a careful and cautious doctor. It's not in me to wing it."

"You need to try something new, but I know you don't want to go out on a limb."

"I sure don't. But if we really did work together cooperatively, it would have a great impact."

"What's that old adage? 'The easiest thing to change is yourself'? If you expect others to change, Graham, you have to show that you're willing to change. If you want others to cooperate, then *you* have to cooperate."

"I *am* committed to change." Graham surprised himself with his conviction. "*How* is the question."

"I think you've got a good system going already. You're talking with Maureen and Serge and me. You're reading articles and books."

"I'm a doctor, not a philosopher. I want to do something."

"A manager complaining about not enough to do? You have lots of opportunities to practice. That's not the problem."

Graham was baffled. "That's the question. What *should* I do?"

"If you want people in the clinic to cooperate with each other," Nora said, "then you have to cooperate with them. That's how you can become a credible leader."

"Sounds nice. But in the heat of the battle, I just don't have the time to sit back and think about how I should act."

"That's often true, but not always. Planning for an important meeting, talking to an employee about poor performance, thinking about how to develop next year's budget—these are all opportunities."

"You know, we might have to reorganize the clinic soon."

"That would be another good time. You said you're going to have to replace the examination tables soon. Why not ask people—doctors, nurses, and maintenance—to volunteer for a task force to decide what examination tables the clinic should buy?"

"It's not that complicated a decision."

"But you want tables that fit your patients, that fit your budget, that fit your maintenance and housekeeping, that fit the nurses and doctors—don't you? Perhaps it's not the most major decision, but it's an important one. And you'd be giving the various people a concrete issue to cooperate on."

"And I wouldn't have to make the decision. But I don't think Helen and Carlos know much about examination tables. It just seems odd to form a special group to make a decision like that."

"Think of it as an experiment. Try it, then see how it goes. Afterward, you can ask yourself, 'Did I set up the task force so that it actually worked cooperatively? Did it accomplish what it was supposed to?' "

"I'm supposed to be running a clinic, not doing a research study! Just coping and keeping my head above water are hard enough when there are so many things going on."

"What's your hurry? You don't have to do everything at once. Do it a little at a time. Getting some 'small wins' is a good way to go." Nora wanted her husband to take a gradual approach to becoming a leader. But she knew that if he couldn't do something big immediately, he often lost interest. "You can't expect to know all there is to know about leadership and working as a team just like that. It will take practice. It will take experience."

"It won't be easy."

"If it were easy, then you'd have to find something else to learn." Nora smiled broadly. "You have something here that you can keep learning about for a long time."

"Hadn't thought about it that way before," Graham teased. "My mind isn't strange enough to think like that."

"You don't have to do it all by yourself either. You have Maureen, Serge, me, and others to talk things over with. You'll find people at the clinic you can talk with too."

"I can't bother everyone about my problems."

"I enjoy it, and I bet Maureen and Serge do too. Most people like to be consulted."

"Maureen said that she was still learning."

"Learning is a win-win activity. We all learn when we talk over issues and try to be better leaders."

Graham felt relieved, as if he had solved a problem. Yet he wasn't sure he had accomplished much. "I appreciate your help. I need it," he told Nora.

Learn Here, Use Here

Many people have a fractured view of learning. They think that ideas and theories exist in the world of books and classrooms, where people learn to think and talk in new, interesting ways. Actions and strategies exist in the world of organizations, where people get things done. Theory is impractical and not very relevant to the world of action, which evolves from feelings, instincts, and experiences.

Graham wanted to connect his ideas and his actions. He was convinced that improving doctor-nurse relationships in the clinic would have far-reaching benefits for the clinic. He had glimpsed the potential of the theory of cooperation to enhance his leadership abilities and develop productive, enhancing relationships. But was frustrated by the gap between what was and what could be.

His training as a physician was an asset here. He had studied medical ideas and theories and tried to apply them. He recognized, though, that there was a long way between doing research and actually using the findings. His experience as a physician had shown him the need to apply ideas and results sensitively and appropriately. The treatment had to fit the patient as well as the problem.

Graham was also learning through his reading and discussing. Yet to gain a fuller understanding about cooperative work, Graham needed to apply what he had learned. Then he would be more knowledgeable and prepared to use his knowledge more skillfully. Learning about cooperation and applying it are mutually reinforcing steps to becoming an effective leader.

Getting Started

Graham was discovering that he had a lot to learn and needed a lot of support to lead in a new way. In fact, the task of becoming a cooperative leader is too challenging and risky for most people to do alone. Leaders need professional discussions in which they talk directly and honestly about the challenges, frustrations, and opportunities of cooperative leadership. Through discussing, explaining, and teaching, they deepen their understanding of and skills in teamwork.

Leaders plan programs and activities together to strengthen their cooperative links. As they put cooperative teamwork in place, they need to clarify their understanding of cooperation and get encouragement to experiment with plans that are appropriate for their people and situation. Discussions about the effectiveness of previous attempts suggest how plans for future action can be modified.

Leaders observe and give each other feedback. Managers can visit each other's teams and give an informed outside perspective on group dynamics and leadership skills. Leaders think developmentally, weigh toward success, and build upon small wins.

Leaders take a long-term perspective. People do not automatically know how to work together and manage their conflicts. It may take years of work before they are highly skilled and proficient. But the point is to enjoy the progress toward cooperative teamwork, not be downcast about imperfections. Leaders see how they can use cooperative leadership to develop a diverse-positive organization that responds to the changing workforce and that values all people. They work to integrate cooperation with the need for quality improvement.

Leaders should learn along with the other managers who are most interested and skilled in becoming cooperative leaders. Leaders increasingly involve their employees in understanding and applying cooperation theory. They strive so that people throughout the organization are committed to building a cooperative culture, and together they forge appropriate, effective cooperative procedures.

Research on Learning Relationships

David Johnson, Roger Johnson, and other researchers have documented the value of cooperative goals and interaction for learning. A statistical review of more than five hundred studies found cooperative learning to be superior to people working competitively and independently across a wide range of learning objectives. This finding applied to adults as well as children.

The shared goal of learning something new facilitates open discussion and other useful interactions. People discuss and debate issues to clarify their confusions. They critique, challenge, and probe into ideas. They connect present learning with past learning. In cooperative learning, people use higher-level thinking, ask more questions, debate different positions, elaborate their views, and engage in problem solving, all of which help them understand and evaluate the strengths and limitations of ideas. People learn by having ideas explained and by explaining ideas. People learning together produces a rich exchange that is not possible when they learn competitively or by themselves. This applies not only to learning nuclear physics but to mastering cooperative leadership.

Learning together is especially useful for the personal and emotional demands of understanding productive relationships. Cooperative learning encourages the support, feedback, and problem solving people need for personal change. Colleagues provide the emotional and problem-solving support needed to translate the theory of cooperation into personal change. Through his discussions with Maureen, Serge, and Nora, Graham was able to identify concrete new ways to lead that fit him and his situation. Studying and thinking alone would have been much less productive for him in developing solutions.

Managers and employees inevitably discuss and learn from their relationships and conflicts. But discussions can reinforce biases, teach misleading lessons, and undermine their work relationships if, instead of focusing on relationship issues directly, participants complain and gossip with people who tell them they are right and others are wrong. They attribute successes to themselves, blame others for failures, and see relationships in more rigidly win-lose terms. They are less prepared and able to learn useful lessons. But if their colleagues are knowledgeable and direct, they can make use of their reflections to learn vital lessons.

Research has developed the theory of cooperation and competition. It has clarified concepts, showed how the theory can be applied in concrete settings, and identified the dynamics and consequences of cooperative and competitive goals. Graham thus needed the help of others to apply the theory, just as he needed their assistance to understand it.

Learning to Use Cooperation Theory

Guides for Action

- Begin the move toward cooperation with yourself.
- Discuss the theory of cooperation with your colleagues.
- Begin with "small wins" to develop your confidence and competence.
- Brainstorm with friends and colleagues how you could make your leadership more cooperative and effective.
- Implement and assess the success of your plans to build cooperation.
- Accept the emotional support you need to take risks.
- Involve your employees so that they become partners in enhancing the organization's teamwork.

Pitfalls to Avoid

- Putting learning and acting into different worlds.
- Applying cooperation theory by yourself.
- Telling people to change.
- Complaining that other people must become cooperative before you will.
- Learning cooperative leadership as a competitive edge over your peers.

PART THREE

Learning on the Job
Applying Cooperation Theory

The person who grabs the cat by the tail learns about 44 percent faster than the one just watching.
—Mark Twain

Leaders inspire a shared vision and epitomize central values; they discover new ideas that will help their employees adapt and innovate. But leadership also requires action. Leaders apply ideas as they confront the same issues and problems their group confronts. They earn credibility by integrating their ideals and action. They "walk the walk," as well as "talk the talk."

Leaders begin change with themselves. They do not simply tell employees that they need to change and improve. They eschew projecting an image of total competence and show that they themselves are experimenting, taking risks, accepting feedback, and not blaming. Leaders model the way for employees by showing them how to learn and develop on the job.

Leaders and employees can use cooperation theory to deal with and learn from pressing issues. The chapters in Part Three illustrate how they can face many threats and opportunities, specifically how to help a troubled team feel cooperative, make the most of a shrinking budget, terminate an employee, and lead with the boss and peers.

8

Helping a Troubled Team
Feel Cooperative

The test of leadership is not to put greatness into humanity, but to elicit it, for the greatness is already there.
— *John Buchan*

"Cooperation doesn't always work," Graham said, more seriously than he had intended. He was having another working lunch with Maureen and Serge. Their study group, which met every two weeks, had kept them in close touch with each other and helped them all deal with important work issues. "It's a contingency. It all depends upon the situation. Sometimes it's a success, and sometimes it's not."

Maureen and Serge had already heard that Graham had called for a task force to select new examination tables for the clinic and that it had been very effective. The task force members—doctors, nurses, and maintenance—had taken the initiative, thoroughly researched the alternatives, and purchased two examination tables, one from each of the top two contenders. Now they were testing the new tables under the clinic's work conditions and soliciting employee reactions. Graham shared his pleasure with Maureen and Serge that the task force had not only made a good decision but had broken down stereotypes as people from different groups with diverse backgrounds and styles got to know each other.

With the encouragement of Maureen and Serge, Graham was now trying to build on this success by forming a multi-departmental task force to recommend how to enhance the clinic's computer system. The task force members included finance and computer specialists as well as doctors, nurses, and maintenance people. When Graham asked several of the members how they were progressing, they grumbled and complained that the meetings were too long and lacked direction. The clinic's finance group was insisting on its favorite vendor. Graham had met with the task force to discuss these problems.

The session had turned out, he told Maureen and Serge, to be disappointing. "I'm irritated with myself. I went in trying to be upbeat and positive, but I got frustrated. I thought I could help them deal with their issues. They talked about problems with the vendors, about getting information from departments, about their computer needs, and about finding a good time to meet. It went on and on like this. It was like a jellyfish. I couldn't get a real good handle on any of the problems, much less get to solutions."

"I hope you told them to grow up." Serge laughed. "That's leadership the construction business way."

"Get self-righteous—that always helps," Maureen said.

"Oh, my cooperative team members," Graham teased. But talking and laughing with Maureen and Serge had already lessened his unease.

"How come people find it so easy to blame everyone else?" Serge wondered. "I come from an industry where we specialize in that. 'It's not us electricians—it's the plumbers, it's the carpenters.' No wonder I'm growing old fast."

"'I'm okay—it's all those other folks,'" Maureen echoed.

"'The first thing on our agenda today: Let's complain about everyone who's not here,'" Serge said.

"I was thinking all those things in the back of my mind, but I didn't say them," Graham admitted.

"Confronting people so directly would have been a high-risk strategy," Serge said. "It could have led to real change, or it could have demoralized them more."

They began to brainstorm what Graham could do. Graham could make an executive decision about which vendor to use to make the task more manageable. Or a computer consultant could come in to help them sort through the complexities and give them some structure.

"Guys, we're thinking like old-style managers, not contemporary leaders," Maureen said. "We're trying to solve the problem for the task force, not empower them to solve it themselves."

Graham thought immediately of his experience in the workshop, when he had seen how focused he and other managers were on the task side, not the people side. "It's so easy to think task, of getting the job done," he said.

"That's us—the problem solvers," Serge said.

"We should really be thinking about how we can help *them* do the job," Graham said. "But I don't see how."

"The new examination tables task force seemed to hit it off," Maureen reminded him. "Didn't it?"

"No problem. They got busy and enjoyed each other too," Graham said.

"But there are bigger stakes and more complications in dealing with the computer system," Serge said. "I can see where a group would have bigger problems. Are the people in the computer task force suspicious of each other?"

"They're not at war, but yes, they seem divided," Graham answered. "They have very diverse styles of working and temperament that for some reason have become really frustrating."

"Maybe they're a team in name only," Maureen suggested.

"It's as if they would rather gossip and blame everyone else than talk directly about why they're not working together very well," Serge said.

"'He said this,' 'She said that,' 'He talks too fast and knows all the answers,' 'She's never organized and doesn't even remember starting times,'" Graham mimicked. "I *did* tell them they should cooperate more."

"Remember, they have to believe they have cooperative goals," Maureen urged. "Knowing you think they should think like a team and work cooperatively doesn't make them feel they're really all on the same side."

They continued to discuss how Graham could help the task force members believe there were a cooperative team and be able to deal with problems together. They recalled from their readings that leaders can use a variety of methods, including group goals and rewards, interconnected roles, and common membership, to help team members become committed to cooperative goals. (See Chapter 6.)

Graham didn't know exactly why, but he felt optimistic as his second session with the computer system task force got under way. He told them that he had been thinking about their situation and wanted them to work on themselves as a team. The members were eager to do so because they felt stuck, but they were also apprehensive. What did Graham have in mind? they wondered.

"What I want us to do is to consider you as a team and put aside, for the time being, immediate concerns about the computer system," Graham began. "The way I see it is that you have been struggling to get focused. Last time it seemed to me that the group was blaming other people for their struggles. Now, I'm not saying that vendors and the departments haven't contributed to your frustrations, but I think you have to become an effective team together and accept and appreciate the differences in your work styles and perspectives if you're going to work together, if you're going to meet the many obstacles and challenges before you." Graham could sense some members warming up and others growing more pensive. His reassurance that this session could be informative and fun also got a mixed reception.

But he pressed on. He intended to summarize briefly what he had read and discussed with Maureen and Serge about why the task force should work cooperatively. But his planned brief summary turned into a full-scale lecture. Seeing blank faces, he repeated and clarified his points. This session wasn't going to be as productive and fun as he had hoped, he thought.

Graham welcomed questions as a break from his lecturing, but the questions intensified his fears that the team members hadn't understood his strategy well. How could they cooperate if they were disagreeing? one asked. How could they be creative if everyone just agreed with each other? asked another. To represent their own departments well meant having to compete to get the best system for their department, objected still another.

Then the team members began to debate these issues with each other. Graham at first tried to clarify and intervene, but then, remembering his profitable group discussions at the leadership workshop, he did not. He remembered that it had taken him time to get a feel for cooperation. How could he expect the task force members to understand so much more quickly than he? He began to relax as they talked. They might learn a little and change their attitudes some, he thought. It wouldn't be dramatic but it would be an important result nonetheless.

When asked, Graham clarified that cooperation involves compatible "win-win" goals and that people in cooperation will disagree and conflict. When the meeting came to an end, Graham said, "I don't want to close off debate and discussion permanently. I've learned a lot while debating these issues myself. For me, though, I want to make it easier for you to cooperate. You have a common task, and I want to supplement that by giving you a reward you all share. I'm thinking along the lines of hosting a dinner at my place and a show afterward."

The task force members laughed—almost, it seemed to Graham, for the first time. A dinner party was a rare event at Cedar Lake Clinic.

"Here's the challenge." Graham smiled. "First your group has to demonstrate a quality group process and a high-quality computer solution."

"How can you do this to us, Graham?" joked one team member. "Here we were thinking that you were a real team leader."

They had more questions: How was Graham going to decide whether they had a quality process and whether their solution was a high-quality one? What if it wasn't their fault that they failed to develop a solution? What if one person just didn't want to work as a team and just let everyone else do it all?

Graham didn't have ready answers to all these questions. He reiterated what he had told them originally—that the system had to be within budget, be as effective at integrating the different departments as possible, and be accepted as useful throughout the clinic. All the task force members would have to sign off on the decision. But he would get back to them about exactly how he would determine if their recommendation was of high quality.

"As far as getting people to do their share and work together, that's your responsibility. You'll be rewarded as a group and held accountable as a group. If some people aren't doing their share, then you have to tell them and work with them so that they do. If they absolutely won't, then you can see me.

"You also have to reconcile the different ideas and priorities of the departments. That's your task too. Granted the clinical people want something different from finance, and the lab people want something different from administration. But we must find a solution that we can all support and that will help us work together better. Your task force is the vehicle." That speech, Graham thought to himself, was more effective than his planned one.

"It was useful. It was even kind of fun." Graham had described the session with the computer task force to Nora. "But they asked some tough questions, like how am I going to measure a high-quality solution."

"But that's not a problem only when you use a cooperative task force," Nora replied. "You always need to define what you're shooting for. It was much easier for the task force on new examination tables to believe they would know what a good solution would look like."

"I can see where the task force might need some help."

"Why don't Helen, Carlos, Louis, and you give the task force guidelines from your standpoint? Then ask the task force to make the guidelines more specific so that everyone has the same sense of where this project is going. Your group can also lead by example and show that you can work cooperatively. Also, you could ask the task force to interview the doctors, nurses, and maintenance people about what they want in a computer system. Each task force member should interview someone from outside their own department."

"So the first cooperative task is deciding what the problem is," Graham said.

"The first—and maybe the most important," Nora agreed.

"I could use our agreed-upon criteria in evaluating their recommendation." Graham paused. "It's so easy to try to do things yourself, but it can be so complex to help people do things. No wonder they say leaders have to have patience. I can see why managers often just do things themselves."

"True, but you had fun. Admit it—you enjoyed talking with them about cooperation and working together."

"It was lively. But I can't help wondering how much they really picked up."

"Think long-term," Nora said.

"Once people see the specifics of our budget shortfall, I'm not so sure how many of us will be thinking long-term."

To Empower or Depower

Graham's first reactions to the obstacles the computer system task force confronted was to try to identify and solve them. But the problems seemed slippery, and the complaints of the members numerous. The solution always seemed to lie beyond them; they would wait for other people to step in and take responsibility for a solution.

Yet Graham was able to reorient himself to help the task force feel capable of solving its problems. With the help of Maureen and Serge, he saw the value of helping the team feel more cooperative and thereby empowered to deal with its internal divisions and external obstacles.

If he had hired a computer consultant or taken on the difficult part of the task himself, he would have run the risk of depowering the team. The team members could easily have concluded that they had failed in their responsibility and that they did not have the competence and confidence to get the job done. They would have hung on to their negative attitudes toward each other and would have continued to blame each other and Graham for their failures.

Every group must be able to solve problems, and problems about how its members are working together are particularly vital. The computer system task force members were suspicious of each other and unprepared to voice their concerns and face their divisions. Rather than confront their belief that the finance group was unreasonably stubborn about one vendor, members complained to each other privately and to Graham. Rather than discuss their difficulties in integrating the different agendas of the various departments, they held on to their beliefs, pushed for a solution that made sense only for their department, and blamed others for the lack of progress.

Strengthening cooperative goals is a central empowering strategy that a leader can use to help a group help itself. A group that feels cooperative is poised to confront its internal impediments and external problems. Cooperative work does not dissolve issues but empowers people to deal with them. With strong cooperative goals, people are less suspicious and more prepared to confront the diversity and divisions that they do have. Rather than viewing their differing perspectives and abilities as obstacles, people see them as assets in achieving their common aims. Then they are able to work more effectively to overcome barriers and achieve their objectives.

Ways to Empower

One reason Graham focused on trying to solve the task force's problems for them was that he lacked a clear understanding of how he could help the team feel confident and empowered. It seemed straightforward to him simply to try to find solutions to the team's obvious obstacles. Maureen and Serge helped him see how he could use his understanding of cooperative goals and culture to empower the task force.

Graham had quickly settled on giving a short lecture to help the group understand what a cooperative culture is. But for him, lecturing was neither efficient nor effective. Graham had neither a well-practiced presentation nor a clear enough understanding of the ideas that he could summarize them concisely. More fundamentally, people do not learn the idea of cooperation simply by listening to a lecture about it. They need to discuss and debate it, try to use it, and reflect on their experiences. Cooperative teamwork cannot be grasped all at once.

If learning cooperation theory requires involvement, so too does applying it. Graham may have been convinced that the task force members' goals were highly cooperative, but what counted was how the members themselves believed their goals were related.

People cooperate most effectively when they understand how doing so will promote their own interests as well as those of others, when they see that working cooperatively is rational and contributes to the company's welfare as well as to their own. Then they will feel challenged to voice their opinions directly, deal with opposing views, learn about their jobs, and take pride in contributing to a more effective organization.

Leaders can help team members understand cooperation and feel cooperative by having them discuss and argue the specific ways that working cooperatively will help them. They can critique articles summarizing the theory and research. They read about companies that use cooperative teams and interview people with experience in these teams. Through reading and debate, they confront stereotypes about cooperation. Rather than believe that cooperation submerges individuals, they come to see how it supports individuality and diversity and encourages people to express themselves and develop their specializations. Cooperation implies not harmonious sameness but vibrant diversity.

Graham had to use considerable interpersonal skills to help the task force. He had to be candid that he saw the group's blaming others as an impediment and that they needed to work on themselves as a team. But he also had to be supportive and encourage them that they could do something about their divisions. He was modeling the candid, conflict-positive cooperation that he was arguing the team adopt.

Empowering a Team to Feel United

Guides for Action

- Help the group recognize how its divisions and suspicions get in its way of reaching its goals and realizing its vision.
- Show that blaming people outside the group will not help it succeed.
- Initiate a debate on the nature and uses of cooperative goals.
- Help the team recognize its cooperative links and feel like a team.
- Focus the group on the importance of its goal for the organization and its own members.
- Make the task challenging so that the group needs all its members if it is to succeed.
- Discuss the criteria to be used to judge group success.
- Reward the group as a whole for success.
- Hold the group accountable for lackluster performances.
- Model spirited cooperative teamwork for the group.

Pitfalls to Avoid

- Empowering a team by doing its tasks for it.
- Fixing the problem for the group.

- Showing you are on the group's side by agreeing that others are to blame for its troubles.
- Lecturing the group on the virtues of cooperation.
- Telling the group to feel cooperative and act cooperatively.
- Assuming that because you see their goals as cooperative, the group members will too.

9

Dealing with a Shrinking Budget

The vital habits of democracy [are] the ability to follow an argument, grasp the point of view of another, expand the boundaries of understanding, debate the alternative proposals that might be pursued.
—*John Dewey*

Graham felt he was on the right track now. He could meet the clinic's budget problems head-on by involving his managers and eventually everyone in the clinic. He had not planned to talk to Maureen and Serge, but he mentioned his concerns about the budget spontaneously at the end of a meeting. They both recommended, as had Nora, that he get people in the clinic involved in the process sooner rather than later. Waiting to tell them about the budget would only allow rumors and fears to wreak havoc. He quickly saw their point.

Yet he couldn't help mulling over his misgivings, either. His area managers might not be quite ready to discuss a shrinking budget. They were used to only a few timid fights over who would get the larger increases, not real battles over how to downsize. How could he keep people focused on maintaining and improving quality and strengthening patient care, rather than worrying only about their own predicament and how the new budget would affect them personally? Sheltered from the marketplace, with little business sense, physicians, nurses, and maintenance people would surely come up with strange, half-baked arguments.

Why hadn't he had the foresight to do something about the budget earlier? Now it seemed that he had just been trying to postpone the inevitable. His peers at other Health East clinics had not focused their own clinics' attention on the budget, either. They all hoped that somehow they would be rescued from this trying exercise. But Graham, for one, now accepted that there were too many forces at work behind Health East's budget shortfall. New government and private insurance reimbursements systems, the changing demographics and needs of the market area, and the new philosophy at the head of the Weber foundation that ran the Health East Clinics were all pushing for change. These forces would not just disappear.

There was a stiff silence as Graham met with Carlos, Helen, and Louis. After attending to a few administrative matters, Graham asked them to discuss the budget and his previously distributed memo showing the ramifications of the zero budget increase for each area. Given inflation, the areas would have to make do with less money than last year. Graham was projecting even trimmer budgets for the next two years.

As Graham summarized his talks with top administrators at Health East and described the reasons for the trim budget and his pessimistic projections, he felt better. But the department managers remained somber and glum.

Helen asked how Graham could be so sure that the budget would not be increased. Graham reiterated that the administration was responding to powerful external forces.

Carlos said that these budgets would mean big differences at the clinic and at Health East. How would staff react to frozen salaries and the cutting of positions? "I wish I were older and could retire," he lamented.

"Not all of us can simply retire," Helen said sternly.

Carlos didn't want to pick a fight with the nurse—they had enough problems already. "I wasn't serious about retiring," he assured her. "It was just a way of saying that it won't be easy."

Helen for her part, was embarrassed that she had overreacted. "We may all age fast with a budget like this."

"We're destined to live in interesting times." Carlos smiled.

"Does anyone else get headaches looking at these numbers?" Louis asked. "I thought helping my son with his math was hard, but looking at these numbers is even harder."

Realizing that pushing them to focus on concrete action too

soon could be counterproductive, Graham entered into their bantering. He tried to put a finger on why he was enjoying their venting and laughter. They were coming to terms with the budget and in a way building themselves up as a team to act on it. His investment in building up the department managers as a group now seemed to be paying off. He saw the managers in a new light, and they were beginning to see each other as more open. "I'm not alone in this," he said to himself. "And they aren't alone either."

"It's good that we can laugh about our problems," Helen said.

"We should also probably *do* something about them," Carlos said. "I hate to sound like a pragmatic killjoy, but we need a method of attack."

"Doctors—practical?" Helen teased.

"We are, though," Carlos replied with surprise. "I always thought, like many people, that being a doctor would be 'professorial,' intellectual. It's taken years of practice and medical school training to reorient me."

"Did you ever get any training to handle a budget like this one? I sure haven't," Louis said.

"No, not that kind of training. This is the school of hard knocks," Carlos said.

"What should be done? Besides retiring and getting training," Graham broke in. He wanted to nudge them into a problem-solving mode. He waited as they considered their reply.

Louis broke the silence. "My guys are going to be suspicious. Anything that we can do to let them know that this is the straight scoop will make our job much easier."

"The nurses will be suspicious too. They'll think they're being tricked again," Helen said.

"The docs just won't believe it. If they do, they'll think it's the clinic's problem, not theirs," Carlos said.

"No wonder we're getting headaches," Louis said.

"We have nothing to hide," Graham said. "Let's tell it to them straight. But we have to make our presentation as constructive as possible."

"We don't want them more confused and suspicious," Louis offered. "We don't want to give the impression that it's management against them."

"At the end they'll have to think that they can do something about it," Helen said. "They shouldn't throw up their hands and give up, or believe that we will or can fix it for them."

"They have to be part of the solution," Graham said. "It's a common problem that we must all face together. I read somewhere that facing reality is one of the first principles of managing."

"It's one of the first principles of medicine, too, but we sometimes forget that," Carlos said.

"We want our patients to face reality, but that doesn't mean that we ourselves do," Helen said.

"Let's brainstorm how we can approach the employees so that they will be willing to face reality and see themselves as part of the solution," Graham said.

They brainstormed for half an hour and began to get a sense of how they could proceed. The essence would be similar to how Graham had approached them. They would meet with the staff, preferably away from the clinic to avoid interruptions, for a couple of hours. They would pass out the projected budget and forecasts, and Graham would lead a discussion on the forces that were causing the budget shortfall. The emphasis would be on involvement; the staff must begin to talk to each other about it. It would be good if people from different areas got to know each other. Louis agreed to talk to a training specialist at Health East for help on designing the budget meeting.

Graham was looking forward to the budget meeting with the staff. But as the day approached, he also grew apprehensive. He talked with Carlos, Helen, and Louis as people gathered for the session, which helped relax him. To make the meeting informal and friendly, they had decided to provide sandwiches and juice as a simple lunch. The meeting room was far enough away from the clinic to provide some distance from everyday demands.

But Graham and the area managers couldn't help noticing the strong, tense expressions on the staff people's faces. The managers weren't sure what these expressions revealed, but it wasn't relaxation.

Louis teased, "Who suggested having this meeting?"

"It seemed like a good idea at the time . . ." Helen offered.

"We've *got* to do it. This will be fun," Carlos said. "We're behind you, Graham."

Graham wanted to project an image of management as serious but approachable. He was not there to threaten them but to challenge them all to confront the budget together.

Graham had planned a well-organized lecture, and he delivered it. He explained the underlying forces operating on the budget, his conversations with the administration, and the basis of his projections. He outlined the implications. He asked that they work with him and the area managers to decide on the tenets that would guide making the cuts. They needed to examine the last three years and forecast future revenues. "Business as usual is impossible. Someone will make those decisions. The issue is whether it will be us or the administration. I prefer us as a team."

Carlos, Helen, and Louis thought Graham's speech was quite effective, though Graham himself was not so sure. As the training specialist had suggested, Graham formed groups of three and asked them to discuss the tenets of the budget cuts together and develop questions for him and the area managers to address.

Although the training specialist had forewarned him, Graham was still surprised that the questions asked him to repeat information that was in his speech and memo. Telling them once had obviously not been enough. Graham tried to follow the specialist's recommendation to answer each question fully, without impatience.

One nurse asked why the foundation that ran Health East and Cedar Lake was getting so greedy all of a sudden.

"Let's put it this way," Graham said. "If you invested ten thousand dollars in a company last year, what would you consider a fair return now?"

People shouted out numbers from five to twenty percent.

"The foundation has been averaging just about a one percent return for the last five years. That's not very good. We wouldn't accept it ourselves."

"But the foundation isn't supposed to be making money. It doesn't need more," objected a maintenance person.

"Is that what you would expect the company you had invested in to tell you at the end of the year?" Graham said. "You'd accept it if they said that you have plenty of money anyway and you're not starving? We need profits if we're going to fund capital expenditures in the future. Banks are putting on the squeeze, too, because they have rewritten loan covenants to protect themselves from bad loans."

"We don't have to grow *that* much," a physician said.

"Times are changing, and we have to change with them," Graham said. "We must remember that the foundation bears great risks. If something disastrous happens here, it will be stuck with having to pass for it. The worst that could happen to us is to not get paid. But the foundation would still have the mortgage, lawsuits, and worse. What if the government changed its reimbursement drastically? The foundation would still have to pay the mortgage and lots of other bills. And the foundation is being asked more and more to support preventive medicine and community development projects."

Graham thought he could see them reassessing their attitudes. Yet there were still surprises. The biggest one was a question asking why Graham was bringing on these budget difficulties. "Our group was thinking that we haven't really had any real fights or difficulties here until now," a physician said. "Now we're wondering why you're giving us these conflicts. Why do you want to agitate us so?"

Graham laughed, but he really was perplexed. In fact, he couldn't believe what he was hearing. He tried to be patient, "I don't think I'm the reason for the budget problem. I'm just the messenger. I plead innocent!" He didn't want to appear to be hitting back.

Louis understood the concerns behind the question more clearly. "Perhaps I can clarify a little," he said. "We're not the reason there's a budget shortfall; those reasons go far beyond us. We are bringing these issues to you. We're not trying to aggravate you, but we want you involved as we try to work out these conflicts."

"You are, whether you want to be or not, part of the problem, but we also want you to be part of the solution," Helen added. "Otherwise, you would be disagreeing and fighting with each other as we tried to live within our budget."

"We managers could make all the decisions ourselves," Carlos said. "Then you could scream and yell at us after we announced the budget. We thought it might work better if we all discussed the issues before we made the decisions."

"We should scream and yell about the budget now?" a staff member called out.

"Let's say debate fiercely," Carlos responded.

"A full airing of our different points of view." Graham smiled.

A physician asked, "Haven't you already made the decisions? You've already passed out your projections."

"Those budgets are just to give us an idea of what will happen to all of us because of our budget shortfall," Graham explained. "Exactly how we will allocate our funds depends upon the decisions we make here. What we need to decide is how to revamp our expenses, yet still deliver quality service to patients."

"But how can *I* make budget decisions?" asked a nurse.

"You alone can't," Louis said. "We have to do it together."

"But we won't be able to get what we all collectively want," said a physician. "You've already told us there will be a shortfall."

"That's where the conflicts come in," Carlos said. "We aren't Santa Claus. Nobody is going to get what they want."

"It's an on-line team-building exercise," Helen said.

Graham explained that he and the area managers thought the most practical way of proceeding would be for people in each area to discuss budget tenets and elect a representative to be on the clinic's budget task force. This task force would become the clearinghouse for suggestions regarding the budget and will make recommendations to Graham and the area managers.

"But our representatives won't be making the decisions—you will be," said a physician sharply.

"We discussed this at some length," Louis replied. "We feel that we are still the ones who are responsible and who will be held accountable for the decisions. The task force must persuade us, but we make this pledge: We're going to be very open to their suggestions and will not go against their recommendations without good reason and without defending our position."

"The task force will be real," Helen said. "It's not an exercise."

"Let me add that if we develop a plan by which we can still be effective with diminished resources—and even more effective—the administration will notice," Carlos said. "I think the administrators will be more inclined to give us additional resources if they see us using the ones we have efficiently and successfully."

Building Cooperative Goals on Scarcity

Graham was learning that if the clinic were to operate as a cooperative team, it would have to confront the complex, troubling task of dealing with its budget shortfall together. He had hesitated to involve people because he sensed that doing so would be difficult and filled with pitfalls. He had assumed that the budget shortfall would place people in competition with each other and that they would have tough, emotional fights over it. That is, he assumed they would have to compete over scarce resources. He would be obliged to try to keep the fights under control and arbitrate who was the victor. Perhaps, he had originally thought, it would be best to avoid this quagmire altogether and announce the budget one year at a time. Unilateral action might efficiently deal with the problem and let people focus on the task of doing their jobs under trying circumstances.

Nora, Maureen, and Serge had reminded him that he did not have to manage the budget crisis alone. He could first involve the area managers and work with them to develop realistic plans, which is what he did. Graham now saw that his leadership could help make the budget crisis a common challenge to which all could contribute. People at the clinic could come to see that the budget shortfall heightened their cooperative dependence upon each other. A focus on their cooperative goal of using the budget shortfall to aid long-term effectiveness would help the clinic people get where they wanted to be. They would become a trimmer clinic that was even more devoted to high-quality patient care.

The clinic was now at a critical change point. If effective decisions were made, the clinic, staff, and patients would benefit for years. But if the budget shortfall precipitated competitive fights over diminished resources, only a few "victors" might gain, but not the clinic people or their patients. Such poor decisions threatened the success of the clinic and thereby everyone's sense of pride and security. They had to rethink their mission, reexamine their activities, and question their merit. Out of these debates could come a stronger, more focused clinic.

The broader the view they took and the longer the time horizon, the more cooperatively the clinic people would see the budget issues. Indeed, if together they created effective ways to develop, implement, and monitor budgets, top administrators might be more willing to invest in the clinic in the future.

Graham and the area managers recognized that the clinic people themselves would have to accept the budget shortfall as a common challenge. It would not be enough for one or two individuals to arrive at this conclusion themselves. The conclusion would have to be a shared one. The clinic people would not work cooperatively on the problem if they believed others were competitive. They would fear that they would be exploited by competitors willing to gain at their expense.

Open Forums for Effective, Fair Work

The clinic people's shared conviction that the budget shortfall was a cooperative challenge would have to be complemented by their confidence that together they could reach their goal. People are motivated to reach even highly desirable goals only when they believe they have a reasonable chance of attaining them. Graham's leadership challenge was to help the clinic people believe that by combining their ideas and suggestions, they could arrive at very effective decisions.

The belief that they had the knowledge and resources to make effective decisions would help them feel confident. To feel highly confident, they also needed to believe that they had the skills and relationships necessary to transform their ideas and insights into workable solutions. Unfortunately, previous managers had given them few successful joint efforts that could reinforce their confidence in each other.

The clinic people wanted to believe that their cooperative effort would be fair, as well as effective, before they committed wholeheartedly to it. They knew that some groups and individuals would lose through reduced budgets, even lose their jobs. Such hot issues raised fears that injustices would be done. Graham had to underline that he would deal with these issues justly.

The open, collaborative approach to solving the budget crisis reinforced the staff's hopes that coping with the budget issues would be done fairly and compassionately. People can accept unfavorable treatment as fair, provided they believe decisions have been arrived at openly and reasonably, not arbitrarily and secretively. The staff was assured that decisions to cut programs or eliminate jobs would be made not by whim or based on personal vendettas but through an open, considered discussion of what was best for the clinic as a whole.

Implicit in this open, participative approach to budget reduction was that decisions would be implemented compassionately as well as effectively. A person in a terminated position would be given a full explanation and the right to dissent and be heard. They would be given job counseling and other assistance to find alternative employment. The needs of individuals would not be neglected in the pursuit of the common good. The next chapter considers the challenge of terminating people fairly and effectively.

Managing Budget Conflicts

Guides for Action

- Help people use the organization's financial information to face reality.
- Show how scarce resources heightens cooperative goals and the need to work together to deal with budget shortfalls.
- Develop ways people can understand the budget, and establish task forces and other procedures to help deal with it.
- Pledge to deal with budget shortfalls effectively and fairly.
- Consider people's recommendations fully and openmindedly.
- Justify your acceptance or rejection of the group's recommendations.

Pitfalls to Avoid

- Assuming scarce resources inevitably means competition.
- Blaming superiors for budget shortfalls.
- Solving budget shortfalls yourself.

- Announcing unilateral cuts in budgets that favor management.
- Relying on the simple principle of identical budget reductions in all areas.
- Showing you are demoralized.
- Protecting people from financial data on budget problems.
- Encouraging unrealistic hopes that budget problems will go away.

10

Firing an Employee

To resort to power one need not be violent, and to speak to conscience one need not be meek. The most effective action both resorts to power and engages conscience.
—*Barbara Deming*

"Strangling an employee—now, that's not allowed by this cooperative theory, is it?" Graham deadpanned to Maureen and Serge.

"That would be stretching its limits, I think," Serge joined in.

"Actually, feeling that you would like to strangle an employee may be within limits, but I would say actually doing it would be a violation." Maureen laughed.

"I'm so frustrated. My so-called accountant, Karen, is driving me crazy." Graham explained that he had told Karen very clearly that he needed an accurate monthly cost report by the twentieth of each month. How could the clinic keep within its budget if it did not have timely information about revenue and expenses?

"Does she have the resources to do it?" Serge asked. "You can't expect her to do it without proper support. She's probably in the habit of preparing these reports three or four months late and no one said anything. Now you change the rules on her."

"The rules have been changed on the clinic, on me, and on her," Graham said. "We've brainstormed what she needs to do on the job. We've upgraded the computer system. We've gotten commitments from people to give her information on time. We've given her assistance. We just don't get the monthly cost reports on time."

"Sounds like you have tried to work with her to solve the problem," Maureen said.

"It hasn't paid off," Graham said.

"I wonder why Karen hasn't responded," Maureen said.

"I wonder how I'm going to get my cost reports," Graham said.

"I guess you're thinking of firing her," Serge said.

"Only wishing. Doing it would be difficult," Graham said. "I'm trying to work cooperatively and get everyone together on this budget issue, but my going out and firing someone could upset the whole cart. Karen's been around for a while and has her friends and supporters. I've already heard some gossiping."

"Firing her would get the gossip and rumor mill really going if it isn't already," Serge warned.

"Gossip can't be ignored, but I don't think you can let it stop you from doing what you have to do," Maureen said. "You don't want people to think you've acted meanly and unfairly. You'll lose credibility."

"True, but I need some resolution. I just can't keep looking the other way," Graham said.

"Keep doing the things you've been doing," Serge said. "You're not acting rashly. You're trying to resolve the issue with Karen. People will respect that."

"It's not your fault she doesn't respond," Maureen said. "You should let people know that you're bending over backward to be fair and give her a chance to respond."

"I've already pledged myself to confidentiality," Graham said. "I've told her that I'm not telling other people in the clinic about our discussions. We have that in our personnel policies."

"Nice gesture, but it doesn't sound like she's being confidential," Serge said.

"No, she's not," Graham said.

"You should check with the personnel department and make sure that you're complying with your policies for discipline and termination," Maureen suggested.

"You think I can fire her and still be a cooperative leader?" Graham asked.

"You're doing this so that the clinic as a whole will be better off, right?" Serge said.

"Yes," Graham said.

"And you're trying to see the problem from her standpoint and to help her respond to the demands of her job, right?" Serge said.

"So I've been good?" Graham asked.

"Sure," Maureen said. "Cooperative work doesn't mean letting someone do her thing while you and the rest of the clinic suffer."

"I don't like feeling so upset with Karen," Graham said. "She has family and friends. She tries—sort of—and she won't take to being let go. But the situation isn't healthy. It's as if she's trying to appease me. But all my talking to her rolls off her like water off a duck's back. She hangs her head down and tells me that things will be all right."

"So how do you like being a psychologist? The new profession suits you," Maureen teased.

"One technique you might try is a written agreement. Write down in black and white what the problem is, what you expect from her, and what the consequences will be if she doesn't meet them. Then you both sign it," Serge said. "You should tell her explicitly that she might lose her job."

"It's going to be hard to be so direct and firm—she'll smile at me and then mope around," Graham said.

"Will it be harder to be firm with her or to do without accurate cost reports?" Maureen said.

"Short-term pain, long-term gain, I guess," Graham said.

"I hope you're not surprised that we're having this meeting." Graham saw the blank look on Karen's face, but he was determined to continue. "Several months ago, we agreed in writing that we would get an accurate cost report by the twentieth of each month. You said that wouldn't be a big problem. But it's September already, and we still don't have July's report. With the clinic under tight budget constraints now, that is completely unacceptable."

"The cost reports don't actually save you money, you know," Karen said.

"I know." Graham tried not to get agitated. "But they can show us how we're doing, identify problem areas, and help us make decisions. I—we—owe that to the rest of the clinic."

"I think we're getting the bugs out of the system and things should improve," Karen said.

"I have heard you say that so often already. The issue I want to bring up is your termination. The best resolution of this is that you leave the clinic. I think you're upset by my continuing pressure on you. I have put a lot of time and energy into making suggestions to you and gotten little payoff. We will give you one month's severance pay, and you can start anew someplace else."

Graham couldn't read Karen's reaction clearly.

"I don't think that the problems are so big," she said. "I'm very surprised that you feel so strongly about it."

Graham didn't want to show his exasperation and annoyance. "I have tried not to surprise you. We both signed the written agreement defining the expectations and the consequences. I'm sorry that you feel surprised now."

"How could you expect me not to be surprised?"

"I can see that warnings are not the same as the actual thing."

"There are many things I do for this clinic."

"I agree. You have contributed much and served us well in many ways. I appreciate it. But the monthly cost report is an essential part of the job that is not being handled well."

Karen paused. "These things get sticky, you know. Grievances. Even lawsuits."

"You have your rights. But I don't see how either of us would win much in a tough fight now. The personnel policies and procedures have been followed."

"I still don't see why getting those cost reports is the biggest thing in the world."

"I know. Your not seeing the need for accurate cost reports in a timely basis has contributed to the situation we're in now."

"I don't know what to say."

"Vera from personnel is prepared to join us now. We can think through the best way for you and us to separate."

"No choice."

"I still don't understand her," Graham said to Nora as they took a walk the evening after he terminated Karen.

"But you did well," Nora said. "You were direct, yet you showed sympathy. I like the way you didn't let her get you off your game plan. You knew what you wanted to do, and you did it."

"Thanks. Our brainstorming about it helped a lot. I just can't figure the woman out."

"She seems like she just tries to get by, ooze out of tough situations in any way she can. It's as if no problem is too big for her to avoid."

"This time she didn't smile much. Before, she would just sort of grin at me and reassure me that things would be okay. Weird."

"She just isn't very good at facing problems, whether it's the cost reports or your demands."

"She's into all this happy talk: 'Think positively . . . Stress kills . . . Be happy.'"

"That's fine, but she doesn't seem to realize that difficulties have to be confronted too. You should be happy with how you handled it."

"Yes and no. Somehow I think I should have been able to find a solution. Perhaps the personnel department could have helped."

"The greatest counselor in the world can't help someone unless that person pitches in and changes. Same with medicine—if the patient doesn't do the therapy, he's not going to get well."

"I did what I could," Graham said quietly.

"What would you do differently next time?"

"Its too hard and too risky for me to terminate someone alone. We should have two people next time, so that I'm not tempted to move away from my game plan, and to help me handle any unexpected crisis."

"Two would also help in case questions are raised and grievances filed."

"Our policy on terminations needs to be updated. It's too general and pie-in-the-sky. It sounds as if we're supposed to do everything in secret. Somehow we have to find a way to maintain confidentiality but also let people know that terminations are for sufficient reason and are carried out fairly and compassionately. An employee grievance committee could make recommendations, and people who have been disciplined or terminated could file a grievance."

"One problem is that Karen more or less had to work alone, without being part of a team. She had only you and your secretary to turn to for support."

"I guess we should rethink how we spend our accounting dollars. Maybe we should pool our resources with other Health East clinics."

"Why don't you ask Karen to stay in touch? That would show you're still interested in her, and you might feel better knowing how she's doing."

"I'd like that. I am concerned about her, but I really believe that her staying at the clinic is not good for her or the clinic."

"You never know. She might learn some things through all this and end up in a better spot. I hope you and Karen both learn from this experience."

"That would be good."

The Imperative to Confront

Graham had felt that he had to confront Karen on her failure to produce the cost reports on time. These reports were critical for him and the area managers in monitoring the clinic's budget performance. Yet he also had doubts and misgivings: How could he confront yet remain a cooperative leader? Might he not lose credibility with other staff members, as well as alienate Karen?

Contrary to popular notions associating cooperation with harmony and "live and let live," cooperation requires confrontation. In cooperation, we want others to perform effectively, for that helps everyone accomplish their cooperative goals. The better Karen did her job, the better off Graham and others would be. Graham supported Karen's efforts and praised her for her successes. However, when Karen did not perform effectively, Graham was frustrated and sought to change her behavior. He first reminded her and inquired, then turned confrontational when her performance did not change.

Graham was reassured by Maureen, Serge, and Nora that he was working for the cooperative good, not just promoting his own individual objectives. His demands and expectations were reasonable; he wasn't imposing his will arbitrarily. He was legitimately requiring Karen to do her assigned, fair share of work.

Graham was also reassured that, at least potentially, he was promoting Karen's interests as well. He wanted her to succeed, and he was working with her so that he could succeed. To keep her on the job, even though she was performing inadequately, would likely have undermined her self-confidence and well-being. She might come to feel frustrated because she had failed to meet her own need to achieve and succeed; she would feel isolated and unappreciated because people did not value her contributions.

Cooperative work actually makes confrontation more likely. In competition, people are "better off" and more likely to "win" when their competitors are performing inadequately. In cooperation, people have a vested interest in helping, cajoling, and demanding effective performance from each other. People in cooperation are much more likely to discuss their frustrations with each other than are those in competition. Our true partners and supportive bosses are those who tell us when we are being ineffective and who work with us to improve.

Effective Confrontation

Cooperation theory suggested how Graham could carry out his confrontation constructively. He had to stay focused on the cooperative goals, even though Karen did not. He had to be patient and disciplined to confront Karen effectively. He had to stay focused on making the situation win-win.

Graham explained to Karen why getting the cost reports would be useful to others at the clinic. He reminded her that everyone relied and counted on his work to be successful and that recent changes had made his work more important and central.

Graham worked with Karen to identify the roadblocks and to facilitate getting the cost reports completed on time. They upgraded the computer system and assured that others would provide her the information she needed. Graham demonstrated that he wanted Karen to succeed.

Graham did not allow himself to get sidetracked or his cooperative intentions to be obscured. He did not criticize Karen as a person, nor call into question her intentions. He recognized her other contributions to the clinic, and he reassured her that she was respected and valued as a person.

Yet Karen had trouble believing that Graham really had cooperative intentions. She thought that he was arbitrary in his demands for the cost reports. She resented what she saw as his badgering and pressuring. She saw his criticism of her cost reports as a more general attack on her contributions and a challenge to her personal competence. But she was unable to voice these concerns to him directly. She left Graham perplexed about her reaction and unable to address her grievances.

Graham not only feared that he would be seen as unfair, he had serious misgivings about the advisability of Karen's termination. Karen showed that she felt she was being done in. Surely, she would suffer embarrassment and inconvenience if she lost her job. She would lose touch with the people who worked at Cedar Lake. She would be thrown onto the job market bearing the onus of a recent termination. Should he perhaps have let her resign? Or given her more than one month's severance?

Perhaps, Graham worried, if he had worked with her earlier or been more skillful, Karen would have seen his cooperative intentions and worked seriously with him to find a solution. Perhaps if he had spent more time with her and built up trust over months of joint work, then Karen would have been more open and prepared to change. He could see the need for a firmer definition of the grounds for her dismissal.

Yet solutions have to be practical. Other people and other tasks were making demands on Graham's limited energy and time too. Graham could not expect himself to be perfect and successful in every situation. In the abstract, conflicts are seldom ever completely "irreconcilable," but in the world of organizations, practical considerations must be considered. On the basis of this reasoning, Graham concluded that his efforts with Karen were not paying off and that termination was a viable, reasonable solution.

It took courage and insight for Graham to fire Karen so directly and cooperatively. Too many bosses let employees' poor performance continue, sometimes for years, or they rely on impersonal, abrupt methods to terminate that leave the fired employee feeling bitter and the other employees ashamed of how their company treats people. Yet as we will see in the next chapter, it was more difficult for Graham to try to work with his boss and peers openly and cooperatively.

Terminating an Employee

Guides for Action

- Establish standards for job performance.
- Confront performance problems directly in a win-win manner.
- Define the problem together with the employee.
- Communicate the benefits of a mutual resolution and the costs of fighting against each other.
- Elaborate the reasons and specific information behind your conclusion that performance is inadequate.
- Listen to the employee's perspective.
- Reaffirm your confidence in the employee, and show respect and acceptance of him or her as a person.
- Create an effective, fair, written agreement that is responsive to the employee's as well as your point of view.
- Terminate only after attempts to problem-solve have proved unsuccessful.
- Communicate the decision to terminate clearly and directly.
- Help the employee accept the termination.
- Communicate your efforts to the organization as a whole without violating the confidentiality or social respect of the employee.
- Appreciate your own constructive motives and abilities in terminating.
- Provide employee assistance programs.

Pitfalls to Avoid

- Hoping inadequate performance will correct itself.
- Making up for months of procrastination by a quick, decisive termination.
- Finding an excuse like reorganization to terminate an underperforming employee.
- Proving that only your views about the employee's performance are valid.
- Jumping to conclusions about the reasons underlying poor performance.

- Assuming your and the employee's goals oppose each other.
- Pretending to listen.
- Prejudging the person.
- Giving up on the person.
- Threatening repeatedly to terminate without following through.
- Softening the blow of termination by implying that the decision might be reversed when it will not be.

Leading with Your Boss and Peers

"What a jerk that Colin is," Graham said to Nora. "As I told Carlos, if that's what that fancy so-called leadership program out east taught him in three weeks, I'm glad he didn't go for four."

"You didn't say that to Colin, did you?" Nora asked. She had been fearing an ugly confrontation ever since Colin had been appointed chief operating officer of Health East and Graham's direct boss six months ago.

"Could have, should have, but didn't. I treated Karen a lot better than he treated me, and *I'm* the one innovating." He explained to her that at the meeting that morning, in the presence of Gerald, the director of Peace Valley Clinic, Ivan, the director of Richdale Clinic, and Dorothy, the director of Elmwood Clinic, Colin had hissed at him for telling some students what he was doing but not keeping Colin and the other directors informed. Earlier in the week, Colin had been on a panel at the university and had been caught off guard when a student asked him questions about Graham's attempts to empower employees. The student had earlier interviewed Graham for a course paper on leadership and had been impressed.

Nora hoped her husband had been apologetic, but she feared asking him directly. "What did you say?" she asked neutrally.

"I told him that I thought it was Cedar Lake policy to be open to requests from the university."

"But that wasn't why he was upset."

"I was just trying to tell him why I did what I did."

Nora painted the confrontation in her mind. It was, in a way, so predictable. She could feel the tenseness in the air and Graham's stubbornness. "What did the other directors say?"

"The only one who came to my defense even a little was Dorothy, and that was only at the end, when she muttered something about being interested in hearing more about what I'm trying to do. Ivan said something smug about why do we have meetings if we're not going to keep each other informed. He loves seeing others get in trouble. Gerald just looked disapprovingly at me. What a cast of clowns I have to work with."

"Tearing your boss and peers down is not going to work. You guys are so tough, so competitive with each other." Nora was frustrated that Graham was repeating his old habits.

"I don't like being slapped in the face. Here I am working hard to make the clinic the best it can be in a time of budget constraints. I'm really trying to be a cooperative leader who makes a difference. What's Colin doing? He makes all these grand noises about 'strategy,' 'total quality,' and 'becoming the industry leader.' He just loves fooling around with his computer program and analyzing the return rates on our so-called investments. He fawns over the latest business guru and talks about how we have to develop our 'competitive advantage.' Words, words, words."

"Graham, when your boss has a problem with you, it means you have a problem."

"He's holding me back—probably jealous of what I'm doing."

"Aren't you being too sensitive and overreacting? Wouldn't you be embarrassed if you had to learn what your people were doing at a public meeting?"

"How was I supposed to know that he'd be there?"

"It's not too much for a boss to expect his people to keep him informed."

"Why didn't he ask me what I'm doing? I'd tell him. He's too busy being a high-flying manager to ask questions."

"Did you tell him any of these things? I hope not."

"I know enough to keep my mouth shut with a guy like Colin. He'd make me pay."

"How come you didn't apologize? That was what he wanted."

"Why should I give him what he wanted after he kicked me in the stomach like that?"

"Lots of reasons. Like your own peace of mind. You can't win a battle with your boss. We have to think about damage control and changing your approach."

The venting had helped Graham regain perspective, and he began to see that he needed to find a way out. He enjoyed feeling superior to Colin, but he also felt himself exposed. "What do you suggest?"

"Begin with an apology. But you must be sincere and direct."

"That would be hard."

"Tell him that in his shoes you'd feel the same way he did. You expect to be kept informed by your people, and you should have kept him informed. You will be right to say it because it's true."

Graham didn't want to admit that he had been stubborn and ineffective, but he could see Nora's point. "Apologizing isn't my strong suit." He laughed.

"It'll be good practice for you." Nora surprised herself with her conviction. "It's not too late to patch things up, but you should begin with a good apology. It will be a cooperative thing to do."

"Cooperative?"

"Yes. You would be telling him that you respect him and his role and interests, and that you recognize that by not apologizing earlier, you were being stubborn and competitive."

"I don't think I was really competing."

"You were determined not to give him what he wanted. You felt frustrated so you would frustrate him. You thought you were losing, and you wanted to win."

"Natural."

"But your boss thinks he was frustrated, and he's only doing his job in telling you to keep him informed."

"Hmm."

Nora suggested that Graham develop a program to keep Colin and the other clinic directors informed about his experiments with cooperative leadership. After brainstorming, they agreed that what would be critical would be to involve the directors in a way that would develop the cooperative links among them and help them become a cooperative team too. At the very least, Graham should avoid intensifying the competition.

Graham became convinced that apologizing to Colin was justified and needed. He told Colin that he was sorry for not keeping him informed, that he understood why he would be surprised and upset by his answer to the student's question, and that he had learned a lesson. Colin could sense Graham's genuineness, and he responded that he might have been too tough and too public in his reprimand. Graham reassured Colin that he had been completely justified and appropriate. They agreed that Graham would distribute some readings and give a short presentation on his work at the next meeting of the clinic directors.

Later, while he was talking with Maureen and Serge, Graham hit on a good idea. He'd have representatives from the task forces on the new examination tables, the computer system, and the budget give short presentations on what they had done too. It would give them recognition and would be a cooperative, team way of making a presentation.

At the next meeting of the clinic directors, Graham briefly summarized the value of involving people through developing cooperative teams. These teams were opportunities to use everyone's knowledge, he said, and to debate opposing views to create high-quality decisions. People also felt more challenged and rewarded, he said. Then the task force members described their careful, thorough work in arriving at recommendations. The clinic directors responded warmly, Graham was moved himself.

Dorothy said, "I'm surprised that there is so much debate and disagreement within these task forces. But these hot discussions don't sound as if they are real roadblocks. Are you really able to overcome them?" she asked the task force members.

"You're always going to have conflict about budgets," said Walter, a budget task force member. "The task force just gives you a forum for discussing them."

"It's one of the reasons working on a task force is so rewarding," said Bonnie, from the new examination tables task force. "We had lots of fun debating and deciding."

"All this takes lots of time," Gerald said. "It's not very efficient."

"Definitely," said Roberta, from the computer system task force. "If you want a quick and dirty answer, don't do it this way. But installing a new computer system and then having people complain and demand lots of changes—that's really inefficient."

"I enjoyed hearing your stories, but sometimes there's no solution that will please everyone," Ivan said. "Some people are just not going to get what they want."

"Agreed," Walter said. "No one got just what they originally wanted in our last budget, but the difference is that this way they had a better understanding of why they didn't. That's critical."

Graham had anticipated that he would be on the spot to answer the clinic directors' questions and respond to their skepticism. But the task force members were able to answer them in a much more direct and specific way than he could. He relaxed and enjoyed the discussion.

Colin enjoyed the discussion, too, but soon he thought they had to move on to more immediate, pressing issues. "Thank you all very much for a stimulating discussion," he said. "We need to empower our employees. Our human resources are probably our greatest competitive advantage. I can see real payback and return in some of these activities. Still, I think we need a more careful analysis of this cooperative teamwork, and of when and when it isn't effective. Still, this was very interesting and a good beginning."

The Need to Manage Your Boss

Graham was learning that he had to take the initiative to build an effective work relationship with his boss and his peers. His failure to keep Colin informed about his innovations grew out of a larger confusion in his own mind that only his boss was responsible for developing a strong work relationship with him. Although Graham knew that his own employees had to contribute to his success, he himself was not committed to helping Colin lead. Graham saw himself taking risks and experimenting within his clinic; within Health East as a whole, it was Colin's obligation to innovate.

Like Graham, many people believe that their boss should take the responsibility to lead because it is he or she who enjoys higher pay and other prerogatives. But developing productive, honest work relationships where people feel they are on the same side and can deal with their conflicts is challenging, and there are pitfalls particular to both bosses and employees. Indeed, bosses need the assistance of employees to lead effectively.

One of the most common pitfalls in the leader relationship is for a boss to assume that he or she must be highly competent about the full range of the issues that confront the group and be able to develop the best answers. Many bosses feel they must demonstrate that they are always right, always in charge, and always in control. They come across as egocentric and arrogant, and it reinforces employee powerlessness. Employees are reluctant to express their opinions and get involved in solving problems if they fear being second-guessed and told they are wrong.

Many employees have the unrealistic expectation that their boss should be the one to begin any discussion of interpersonal problems or conflicts. The boss is in the best position to confront issues and discuss frustrations, employees think, and they fear that they will be seen as complainers if they bring up a conflict. The boss will hold it against them for being the "bad news" messenger or for wasting his or her time.

Such high, unrealistic expectations of bosses on the part of both bosses and their employees obstruct leadership. Few, if any, bosses have the full range of knowledge and insight to make wise decisions about all the complex issues facing most groups and organizations. Today's problems need team solutions. Nor can bosses anticipate or know all the frustrations and grievances that employees have. Bosses cannot read employees' minds or know when and why they feel aggrieved.

The superior status and power of bosses also interfere with this. Some bosses get distracted by their power and fail to see that they depend upon employees. They do not feel that they have to consider the employees' perspectives. Fixated on their own agenda, they bark out orders, demand compliance, and neglect to listen to their employees.

Other bosses feel uncomfortable about having authority and power. They are afraid of being heavy-handed, and in vain attempts to be "participative," they fail to provide needed direction. To avoid appearing nosy, they do not discuss employee problems. To avoid appearing harsh and alienating, they delay confronting employees on inferior performance. Graham learned from his experience that a reprimand from a boss can feel very punitive.

Employees easily underestimate the demands that are made on their boss. Bosses are thought to have it easy in that they get other people to do their work. They have their own offices, secretaries, and other amenities. But nearly all bosses have bosses, too, and they often must deal with complex problems in unsupportive environments. Since they have their own frustrations, they may not be very sensitive to employee needs or very open to dealing with employee frustrations.

Most bosses have technical backgrounds, with little formal education in leadership. They have ill-conceived ideas about the leader's role and are uncertain how to use their own power and authority constructively. They expect that their employees will automatically "cooperate," and they do not invest much in establishing the cooperative relationships necessary for productive collaboration.

Like many managers, Colin had neglected to build relationships with the people who reported to him. Graham thought he could count on Dorothy for some assistance and support, but he thought Gerald and Ivan would prefer to see him fail. Graham was coming to see that it was in his interest as well as the organization's that he take the initiative to create stronger cooperative links between himself, his peers, and Colin.

Strengthening Cooperative Links

Colin had expected that Graham, as his subordinate, would assist and help him, and he was angry when he had evidence that Graham was not. Colin had been publicly embarrassed by not knowing what Graham was doing. He believed Graham had had ample opportunities to tell him informally or in a formal meeting about his experiments. It had been very much Graham's responsibility to do so, Colin thought. In fact, his failure smacked of being secretive and competitive, while his refusal to apologize confirmed Colin's suspicions.

Colin's suspicions had a basis in fact. Graham did feel that Colin was his rival, and he had not reconciled himself to having Colin as his boss. Graham was wise enough to hide his obvious competitiveness, but he couldn't do so completely. Graham also had competitive feelings toward his fellow clinic directors. Although here too he avoided open competition, he thought in terms of building up his own clinic to be better than the other clinics at Health East and in terms of being a better leader than his peers. He quietly encouraged his staff to talk about the Cedar Lake Clinic as the most innovative in Health East. He thought this competition would be a good motivator for the clinic and would help him pursue his own goals.

But Graham could also blame his own competitiveness on Colin's failure to develop strong cooperative goals among the clinic directors. Colin had scheduled regular meetings and talked about improving communication, but he had not systematically encouraged cooperative relationships and collective responsibility. Within this vacuum, the strong-willed, proud directors generally felt rivalrous toward each other and Colin.

Graham had reflected on his conflict with Colin and thereby came face to face with the dangers of this competition. But he also realized that he could do something about it. He could clearly communicate his cooperative intentions to Colin and his peers, and he could act consistently with them. He did apologize to Colin and reassured him that he would not make the same mistake again.

Graham had then developed a plan to share his ideas and experiences with his peers at the meeting. There he gave the clinic directors firsthand accounts of the applications of cooperation theory to stimulate their thinking and planning. Graham's employees had given presentations and made themselves available as resources that the clinic directors could call upon if they wanted to experiment. Both the directors and Colin were stimulated by the presentation, while Graham and his staff people gained recognition for their achievements.

Graham could not expect to change Colin and his peers directly. What he could change was his own behavior. He was determined to be disciplined in acting cooperatively toward them. He would keep them informed, share his experiences, and in other ways show that he wanted them all to succeed. His language would reflect his cooperative thinking. He would have to protect himself from the very competitive Ivan, but he was determined not to get trapped into a rivalry. It takes two to cooperate, he knew, but it also takes two to compete.

Graham also began to consider a more radical innovation: His clinic would become more thoroughly team-based. He saw that he could involve Colin and the clinic directors as partners in this innovation. The next chapter describes becoming a team organization.

Leading with Your Boss and Peers

Guides for Action

- Change your behavior to change your relationships with your boss and peers.
- Appreciate the pressures and problems that your boss and peers face.
- Understand their goals and how you can further them.
- Inform them of your vision and aspirations.
- Identify how your boss and peers like to lead and work with people.
- Make their working with you efficient and enjoyable.
- Keep them posted on your successes and difficulties.
- Show that you appreciate their effort and support.
- Make it easy for them to bring up problems and conflicts.
- Apologize for mistakes, oversights, and slights.

Pitfalls to Avoid

- Believing your boss and peers have much easier jobs than you do.
- Assuming they share your vision and know your goals and problems.
- Assuming you know their visions, goals, and problems.
- Talking to them only when they ask.
- Assuming your boss will initiate a discussion if she is concerned with your performance.
- Believing that you can never confront your boss.
- Believing she gets paid so well she does not need your thanks.
- Telling your boss and peers only of your successes and covering up your failures.

PART FOUR

Deepening Competence

Continuous Development

> *Through self-development comes the confidence needed to lead. Self-confidence is really awareness of and faith in your own powers. These powers become clear and strong only as you work to identify and develop them.*
> —James M. Kouzes and Barry Z. Posner, The Leadership Challenge

The status quo is an illusion. At any given time, leaders and their groups and organizations are either becoming more in touch and more synergistic, or they are becoming more fragmented and ineffective. Leaders can have a long-term impact by developing team organization, in which groups rather than individuals are the basic building blocks. Team members encourage and cajole each other to complete their common assignments and reach their mutual goals. They support each other's learning and development.

Not only can leadership be learned, it must be. Leaders model the way by exploring ideas and taking risks. They strive to work and manage their conflicts cooperatively as they urge others to be a team. Leaders realize that becoming a leader is a lifetime pursuit; they commit themselves not to perfection but to ongoing growth, both as leaders and as people.

12

Team-Based Organizations

When you are playing with a group of guys, as opposed to a single sport, it's different. You can play tennis and win a championship and know you've accomplished something. But when you can look in the eyes of teammates and can share that feeling, it's something you can't describe.

—*Bryan Trottier, Pittsburgh Penguins hockey team*

Graham was still surprised, he told Nora, by how invigorating an apology could be. He had genuinely apologized to Colin, and then he had used the opportunity to present himself, his people, and his ideas in a good light to the other clinic directors. Since then, he had felt some of the tension between him and Colin and the directors dissipate. Nora was right—tearing down your boss and your peers is a no-win proposition. He was proud that he had landed on his feet.

Graham also felt empowered that he could lead the clinic to tearing down its internal barriers and building a thorough team organization. He envisaged physicians and nurses sitting down face to face to discuss in concrete terms how together they could provide quality service to patients, keep costs down, and manage diversity. The technical and laboratory personnel and the maintenance people would feel like important members of the clinic. He and the other managers would no longer be putting out fires and listening to complaints; they would be challenging and guiding. People would be supportive and honest with each other. He would leave a powerful, long-term mark on the clinic.

Graham's enthusiasm propelled him to forge a new organizational chart. To make the clinic more open and responsive, he would reduce administrative layers and create teams that would be self-managing. He read about self-management teams and companies experimenting with them. He visited Brian Hamilton, whom he had met at a local health-care association luncheon and whose organization had been working toward self-managing teams for three years.

Graham was determined to push forward, but his discussion with Brian gave him second thoughts. Brian said that his organization was still adjusting to the team structure, had not yet fully realized its potential, and had only one or two self-directing teams. Brian told Graham a story of the turmoil and turnover of the organization's move toward teams, a story that Graham found sobering. Graham had hoped to unveil a full-scale plan of the new organization to the area managers and then the staff of the clinic. But now he thought it better to ask the managers to help him sketch in and enhance his plan.

Carlos, Helen, and Louis welcomed the challenge of redesigning the clinic's organization. They debated how many administrative layers were desirable and who would belong to which self-managing teams. They discussed how to develop a set of principles that they could clearly communicate and defend. Now Graham was feeling more confident that they were on the right tract.

At the beginning of their second planning session, Louis said, "It's a beautiful plan, but the doctors won't go for it. I can't see how they will accept the loss of status. I can hear their objections already, about how the new approach makes them less able to do what they believe is right yet they are still held accountable."

The area managers turned to Carlos for a reply. "There will be some, perhaps even many, physicians who will have questions," he said. "Maybe even a lot. We will have to persuade and cajole. There is definitely a selling job here."

"To be fair, the doctors won't be alone," Helen said. "Nurses can be very conservative too. They have been brought up in a hierarchy, and some of them are very comfortable with it. Others will doubt that the doctors really want to 'step down to their level' and discuss openly with them when they—the doctors—have things pretty much their own way now. Why should they change?"

Louis said, "My people don't have much status to lose. They should be the most open to this kind of change. But they too are part of the existing system, and they will be skeptical. I hate to say it, but some of them take pleasure in casting the physicians as villains. Now who are they going to blame?"

"They blame the doctors?" Carlos said, surprised.

"Sure," Louis said. "Whenever we have a budget problem, it's because the doctors are taking too much money. When nurses complain about poor housekeeping standards, my people gripe that the nurses never pick up after themselves."

"But why should the housekeepers complain? They're paid very well compared to other industries," Carlos said.

"I don't hear them grumble that much," Helen said.

"You don't hear them speak, but that doesn't mean they don't talk to each other," Louis said.

"Great way to run a clinic." Graham shook his head. "Who'd want to run any organization like this? Who benefits?"

"Not the patients," Helen said.

"Not us managers," Louis said.

"What keeps it going?" Carlos asked.

"Honestly," Louis said, "I think my people feel better when they can blame physicians and bring them down a notch or two."

"That feeling can last only for a while, though," Graham said.

"Everyone loses in the long term," Helen said. "Trouble is, few people think long-term."

Graham was slowly resigning himself to revising his plans and his schedule. Moving to a team organization would not happen quickly. "Our plan assumes that people want to and will work cooperatively with us and with each other. We know intellectually we can't make that assumption, but somehow it took our discussion to remind us of the simple truth that we must develop the cooperative relationships throughout the clinic if we're going to succeed."

"We've been working together, talking, and discussing issues for some time, so we have a fair amount of cooperation among ourselves," Carlos said. "But we can't assume that the people who report to us will have the same attitude."

"In their defense, they haven't had many opportunities to really discuss and work together closely," Helen said. "Mostly, they stay within their own groups."

"People need an opportunity to get involved with each other so that they can see the benefits of working cooperatively," Louis said.

Graham asked them to discuss how they could proceed with their plan, given these mistrustful attitudes and the clinic people's lack of experience and skills in working together. They all came to see that it was critical for them to develop cooperative, open-minded relationships. But they were stymied about how to proceed.

"We have another problem," Graham said. "We need to keep the other clinics informed and supportive too. We want the directors and people of the other clinics cheering us on. That way, this team idea might spread to those clinics someday. If it just stays with us, the administrators might decide one day that we are too strange and unusual."

"Talk about bad attitudes," Helen said. "There's not much trust between the clinics either."

Then Carlos mimicked Dorothy with her well-known, full-teeth smile and her high-pitched voice; "'We're so happy to support you in your efforts. It's too bad that you're not as supportive, warm, and lovable as we are at Elmwood. Perhaps it's a problem you were born with.'" The other area managers broke into smiles, then laughter.

Helen took the dour persona of Gerald. "'You guys try hard, but how come you're so unprofessional? We work with the university hospital and are in touch with the latest research and wizardry. You still practice blood-letting.'"

"How about Ivan?" Louis said looking down his nose. "'Why do you bother with Band-Aids and counseling? Practice medicine, not psychology!'"

The managers embellished their characters and laughed louder and louder. They had switched from making a serious assessment to releasing laughter.

Graham kept saying, "What a way to run a organization," but instead of getting somber, he laughed louder.

"Who says you have to watch TV to laugh?" said Louis. "Just look around. What could be wilder than reality?"

"It's a tragedy and a comedy all rolled into one," Helen said, wiping her eyes.

"Someone should write a book on us—but people would think it was fiction," Carlos said.

"Funny situation, strange situation. . . . We might as well laugh about it," Louis said.

"Really funny. But not funny, too," Graham said.

At the next study group meeting, Graham brought Maureen and Serge up to date on his efforts to make the clinic team-based. "We've had some success working cooperatively," he said, "but still there's lots of suspicion among different groups and too little experience in working cooperatively."

"It sounds as if you've done a good job of bringing your managers along so that they want to work cooperatively," Serge said.

"Now the challenge is to do that throughout the clinic," Maureen said.

"I could meet with the staff in small groups to discuss my ideas about working more cooperatively," Graham suggested.

"Perhaps a day retreat, where people talk about what cooperation is and how they can use it at Cedar Lake," Maureen said.

"You could distribute some reading beforehand," Serge said. "Have people debate working cooperatively, and even have them do skits that show how their groups are or are not working cooperatively."

"There are some cooperative simulations that people could participate in to get some experience and to see the benefits and fun of working cooperatively," Maureen said.

"But just because we debate cooperation and get some experience in it doesn't mean that we will do it," Graham said.

"What would be good, though, is that people would be learning together as a team about cooperation and deciding together if they want to work cooperatively," Maureen said.

"Like we read in that book. It sounds strange, but it might work, too," Graham said.

"You'd be learning more about cooperation, getting a realistic picture about whether people in the clinic really want to work that way, and in the process perhaps getting their commitment," Serge said.

"You'd be checking to see whether the doctors really are arrogant and really don't want to work with nurses," Maureen said.

"If they all saw that they could cooperate in learning, putting on skits, and playing the games, and and if they could agree that they want to work cooperatively, then you'd be a lot further along than if you kept trying to sell and persuade."

"That kind of discussion and learning from experience could help dissolve some of the mistrust between the groups, too," Serge put in. "If the doctors say they can't trust the nurses, then they could discuss why and begin to work out of it."

"There might be lots of conflict and bad feelings," Graham said.

"You already have conflicts and bad feelings," Serge said. "This debate just gets them out into the open, where people can do something about them."

"But you do agree that there are risks involved in having such a workshop," Graham said.

"I do. But there are risks in not having it, too," Maureen said. "The groups will continue to stand apart from each other, and it will be difficult to innovate."

"So maybe this workshop would be a practical way to proceed," Graham said.

"It could be powerful," Maureen said.

Getting Prepared

Graham was convinced that becoming a team-based organization would help the clinic deal with its pressing issues and make it a more meaningful place to work. It would be a win both for the organization and for the staff. But he was learning that he couldn't translate his own convictions and sense of urgency directly into practice. Just because he was convinced and understood didn't mean that the clinic staff did. Nor did understanding in itself mean that behavior would change.

Graham was rediscovering the adage that leadership means getting people to want to do things that need to be done. The people at the clinic, not just Graham, had to be convinced that becoming a team organization was critical both for them and for the clinic.

Lively discussions and experiential learning can help people feel an urgency about becoming a team organization. Rather than merely tell and sell, group discussions deal directly with objections and reservations. It's not enough to get people's acquiescence and compliance; they have to become internally committed.

Experiences in cooperation help people understand it. An open-minded, full discussion about what cooperative teamwork is and its potential value for the organization, putting on skits about the teams, and doing cooperative games are concrete examples of lively cooperation. People thereby gain confidence that they can work as an effective team.

Graham had a vision that the clinic would become a team organization. In Graham's innovation, teamwork was both the means and the end. Through spirited teamwork, the clinic people would become a team-based organization. The method would reinforce the message. They could use the challenge of becoming a team to gain valuable experience in teamwork. Although he at first wanted to make it happen quickly, he was learning that the processes of becoming a team organization could be valuable and enjoyable. They would learn and enjoy themselves as they debated and moved toward becoming a team organization.

Moving to Teams

Graham's plans called for the clinic people to get exposure to the idea of cooperation and to appreciate its power and usefulness. Reading books and articles, getting involved in discussions about teamwork, attending seminars and presentations, and talking to people who were already using teamwork and the cooperative model would help them to explore the issues still further. Their involvement in a clinic task force could be the most convincing experience of the value of working cooperatively.

Graham thought he could use workshops and discussions. He could begin by describing his vision of a cooperative team organization. Working in groups, others would discuss this vision and give their input. They would ask questions, emphasize certain points, and fill out the meaning that the vision had for them. They would discuss how teams could further the business vision, improve customer service, and make the organization a more secure and meaningful place to work. Graham hoped that they would embark on becoming a team organization because they understood that it would pay off for them and the clinic.

Common Knowledge

Graham wanted to ensure that people were on the same wavelength in their commitment to strengthening the team. He wanted them to have a shared set of aspirations for it, even though they might have opposing ideas of how specifically to create that kind of team.

He wanted them to challenge their outworn stereotypes that working cooperatively means harmonious sameness and come to understand that cooperators might appreciate and use their differences and conflicts. Their lively discussions about cooperation theory would be concrete experiences of productive teamwork.

Mutual Work

At future workshops and meetings, Graham could encourage people to take joint action to strengthen themselves and the organization. People could form task forces to recommend a more compelling vision, suggest group goals and shared rewards to strengthen feelings of being united, identify training and opportunities that could empower people, create ways that opposing ideas could be used to explore issues, and suggest how people could learn to manage their conflicts and learn from their experiences.

They could work to achieve a living, workable consensus on the company's direction. They could structure job assignments, rewards, and norms to strengthen cooperative goals. They could refine communication and productive conflict skills to feel confident and prepared to work together. They could use conflict to identify and solve problems. They could reflect on their experiences, celebrate their successes, and use their learning to strive for ongoing improvement.

Ongoing Development

Once they recognized the need to continue to invest in their groups and organizations, or else risk creating suspicions and perpetuating unresolved hostilities, people could commit themselves to dealing with conflicts directly and openly. They could schedule regular sessions to reflect on how they are working together and to decide how they could strengthen their cooperative links.

They would realize that their teams are either becoming more united and effective or else more fragmented and ineffective. They could commit themselves to ongoing renewal to strengthen their cooperative bonds and spirited teamwork.

The clinic people could help extend cooperative teamwork to the other clinics. Their teamwork would be more powerful if all the Health East clinics were supporting and helping each other. Otherwise, the other clinics might question Graham and his clinic as embarking on a dangerous course, or they might fear they were being cast in the role of traditionalists, out of step with current practice. Graham would feel more supported if his peers and Colin were themselves convinced that cooperative teamwork was valuable and became partners in a common enterprise of making Health East a team-based organization.

Becoming a Team Organization

Guides for Action

- Make a personal, vigorous statement of your own conviction to teamwork.
- Make the means of change consistent with the end of teamwork.
- Model the way by using cooperation theory to deal with important issues.
- Admit it when you and your colleagues fall short of the ideal.
- Provide background reading material.
- Structure discussion and debate.
- Encourage people from all ranks to speak their minds.

- Openmindedly explore the limitations of your model of team-work.
- Allow people the time and opportunity to explore issues and to change.
- Express your conviction that the organization can strengthen itself.
- Develop a shared set of beliefs about how the organization should operate as a team.
- Use task forces and other forums to explore specific issues and make recommendations.
- Realize that becoming a team organization requires the commitment and hard work of gradual, continuous development.

Pitfalls to Avoid

- Assuming everyone has the same definition of cooperative team-work.
- Insisting on quick agreement and action.
- Expecting everyone to agree with you.
- Taking all criticisms as narrow-minded resistance.
- Taking all doubt as lack of interest.
- Assuming no one agrees with you.
- Building yourself out of the organization as superior.

13

The Business as the Business School

It may be that the true antithesis of "leader" is not "follower," but "indifference," i.e., the incapacity or unwillingness either to lead or to follow. Thus it may be that some individuals who under one situation are leaders may under other conditions take the role of follower, while the true "opposite" is represented by the child who neither leads nor follows.

—L. Ackerson

"Excellent! A very gratifying and useful experience," Graham responded to Maureen and Serge's queries about the feedback he got on his leadership style. At their urging, Graham had asked Carlos, Helen, and Louis to complete a questionnaire about his leadership, and after Graham reviewed their responses, they had all discussed Graham's leadership together.

"I was apprehensive at the beginning about getting feedback," Graham told Maureen and Serge. "What surprised me was how eager I became, the more we got into the feedback. The most difficult part was knowing how to proceed and getting the process started."

Graham had combined a few questionnaires on leadership and cooperation and classified the questions as "Credible," "Knowledgeable," "Doing It," "Promoting It," and "Learning." "Credible" questions were those that asked how much Graham conveyed he was committed to developing productive work relationships and how much he followed through by making cooperative work a high priority. "Knowledgeable" questions were those that asked how well Graham understood what it means to work cooperatively and knew the existing conflicts and had other abilities for leading people to work effectively together.

The "Doing It" questions asked to what extent Graham himself was working cooperatively by seeking mutual goals, exchanging ideas and resources, and sharing rewards. "Promoting It" probed the extent to which Graham was helping groups work cooperatively. Was Graham helping to develop a team organization? Did he assign group tasks, give common rewards, assist them in developing forums and skills to work together, and celebrate their joint successes? "Learning" questions focused on Graham's experimenting and risk-taking to become more effective. They also asked for an evaluation of Graham's overall impact as a leader and the clinic's effectiveness as an organization.

"Well, what did they say?" Serge asked with a smile and with interest.

"I was surprised, but at the same time not surprised by their feedback," Graham said. "The consensus was that I get high marks for learning and trying to change. I can see now why they think that way, but I thought maybe they didn't appreciate my taking risks."

"I bet you came across as credible," Maureen said. "You've been working hard on that."

"True, they saw me as credible, but they said I could be more vocal about the need to work cooperatively throughout the organization. Just saying it once in a while isn't enough. I need to keep reinforcing."

"That's useful feedback," Maureen said.

"They said they felt I was knowledgeable, too, about what it means to work as a productive team. They especially liked that we were able to separate cooperation from conflict and everyone thinking alike. Again, though, they thought I could discuss and share this knowledge more often and more explicitly.

"'Doing It' was mixed. They saw me discussing issues with them and working with them for common goals. My weakest area—and again, I could see the point after they made it—was that I don't give enough recognition and praise. It brought home to me that we need a task force on how to to recognize people more and also hold them accountable. I can't do it alone.

"As far as 'Promoting It,' they saw themselves as a group making progress and off to a good start with the whole clinic. We're getting more group tasks, but we still have precious few concrete common rewards. Again, they thought my weakest area was celebrating joint successes. I'm not an emotional kind of guy, and it shows. It feels awkward to me to smile and pat people on the back. I don't want to appear condescending, either."

"It's interesting that these 'hard-driving' professionals want more emotional support," Maureen said.

"What also came across loud and clear is that they want more support from me for their own development as leaders," Graham said. "We spent more time on that than on anything else, and that's where they saw me as most lacking. They want me to help them be more effective cooperative leaders."

"Just the right kind of criticism," Serge said.

"It is?" Graham asked.

"They want more of your leadership, not less," Maureen observed.

"They want you to give away your approach," Serge said.

"That works well, because as you teach them to lead cooperatively they're helping you lead cooperatively too," Maureen said. "Definitely win-win."

"Do you mean that the area managers and I should have more feedback sessions?" Graham asked. "We could focus on each manager and give him feedback, for instance."

"Why not?" Maureen said. "You can read and discuss leadership and cooperation and help each other develop and follow through with working with their teams. You can help lots of people become leaders, and that will help you lead."

"Supervisors and work teams can discuss leadership and cooperation and decide how they can improve their teamwork," Serge said.

"That would be quite a 'team learning' organization,'" Maureen said. "You'd have groups like ours throughout the clinic. It'd be great."

"Yes. . . . Your plans for me never seem to end," Graham said with a laugh. He was excited about these leader support groups, yet he couldn't helping wishing that he had somehow already arrived and could take a breather from all the experimenting. He knew that wish was unrealistic.

"You don't want us to think about how to redo your house, do you?" Serge said.

"What are friends for if not to give some help along the way?" Maureen said. "But we have forgotten something."

"More plans?" Graham teased.

"I know one thing," Serge put in. "Why don't you have your boss complete the questionnaire and discuss your leadership with him? It would be interesting, and you might get him more tuned in to cooperative leadership and helping you lead."

"Good idea," Maureen said. "But what we've forgotten is to celebrate your getting feedback and your achievements that the area managers saw."

"Way to go, Graham!" Serge said.

"Serge and I will plan a special celebration," Maureen said.

"That would be nice," Graham said with simple candor.

"Now I know why I took my job," Graham said to Nora that evening.

"Tell me," Nora said. She had enjoyed watching her husband become more open and reflective.

"Putting it into words is difficult. . . . Yet somehow all this seems relevant," Graham began. "I went into medicine because I wanted to do something that was clearly a good thing to do. Helping people be healthy—who could argue with that? I would have a set of skills, a mastery of an area that I could get my hands around. I would be a doctor who knew how to do specific, useful things, and I really wouldn't have to depend upon other people. I would be in charge. People would come to me, and I would apply my skills to help them get well."

"I remember—you were a very optimistic medical school graduate," Nora said.

"Times were good, and my future seemed assured. But I soon learned that I wasn't in complete control of my destiny. It was hard to face the fact I couldn't help some patients recover. But even the patients I could help, I had to learn to work with them. Just telling them what treatment and therapy to take wasn't enough. I had to earn their trust. It took lots of effort, but I came to like developing these relationships."

"I remember you did a lot of soul-searching about what it means to be a doctor and how you should treat your patients. In the end, you had many loyal patients. That meant a lot to you, I think," Nora said.

'When I got more specialized and began at Cedar Lake, I had a whole group of other people to work with. I knew most of the other docs, but nurses and administrators were more difficult. They weren't docs, but they weren't patients, either. I shudder sometimes to think of the fights I got into, the demands I made, and the insults I used. It wasn't easy being my boss or coworker.

"No, it wasn't easy working at the clinic, and there was a lot of mistrust and hostility. But you came to respect the nurses, and they you."

"We had some good times. Funny—when you look back, you see things that you didn't see so clearly then. Though I used to complain so much, working with other people, getting to know them is what I remember most vividly and fondly."

"That's my experience too."

"But you seem to appreciate your relationships more immediately than I do."

"That may be true, but I've had to learn too."

"So taking this job as clinic director was just the next challenge of working with even more different kinds of people. It's quite a leadership challenge to develop an organization in which diverse people work together."

"You've come a long way."

"I've had to give up this notion that I alone could control my fate by having doctor skills. Even doctors have to work with patients and people to be successful."

"Even doctors have to change."

"Really. That confident medical school graduate never dreamt that he would have to change and learn so much."

"And change is another reason you have to work with other people."

"Certainly to lead. But for new medical skills, too, even for maintenance, you have to be continually discussing and learning from each other. Louis was saying that he needs to hire people who have proved not only that they can work with others but that they can learn new systems with them."

"It's a fast-changing world, and it's going to keep on changing."

"There's no getting off this rocket. I hope our kids have gotten the message. None of this serving hamburgers at the local fast-food place as a career choice."

"They're conscientious students, and they seem to listen when we talk about how they must be prepared to face a tough, unforgiving job world. But some of their friends seem to live in a fantasy that having a job that gives them enough money to buy a car is all they really need."

"It's scary. I think there're quite a few people at Cedar Lake who still haven't gotten the message about how much we're going to have to change, how powerful the forces for change are."

"Change is more built into the ideas and myths of a consumer products company like mine, so we may be more prepared."

"Colin was saying that the budget may actually be worse than we anticipated. I'm glad we've invested in our relationships, because they're going to help us through the turbulence. Pity the organization in which people are still fixed on working against each other."

"It's funny that our relationships can be our stabilizers, can help us feel that we can, if not control change, at least manage and be on top of it."

"We'll certainly feel more confident if we believe we can face our budget problems together. I don't see how I could effectively cut the budget by myself."

"That's a big change from thinking that if you knew doctor skills, you'd be in charge of your destiny."

"Sometimes the simplest truths are the most difficult to get to."

"And you need friends, as well as good ideas, to get to them."

"I've had my friends." Graham paused. "You've been great, honey. Thanks."

"My pleasure. I've learned a lot too and enjoyed watching you be challenged, take risks, and become a leader." She laughed, "You've been a good student of leadership."

"I've needed to be."

Building Our Organizations

Graham and his colleagues were confronting the reality that old ways of leading and working are increasingly dysfunctional. They were groping for alternatives to the traditional hierarchical, individualistic, and conflict-negative ways of organizing. But debunking authoritarian methods has proved to be much easier to do than actually transforming our organizations for today's world. Graham and the staff at Cedar Lake Clinic were rediscovering a long-standing but often overlooked truth: that productive relationships are the foundations of organizations that work.

The traditional hierarchical organization assumes that mechanical, impersonal cooperation is effective. Tasks are broken down into small parts; people are hired and trained to perform these tasks without being encumbered with the need to collaborate. To solve problems and end conflicts expeditiously, managers select and implement solutions. People are expected to treat their work, difficulties and colleagues without emotion and favoritism.

Facing Reality

The quickened pace of today's marketplace, continuous technological development, an increasingly diverse workforce, and major shifts in people's expectations have exposed the inadequacy of the assumptions that underlie the hierarchical organization. Developing a new product quickly and accomplishing other important contemporary tasks cannot be completed by individuals working alone and coordinated by a boss. People need the active support, involvement, and competence of specialists from many areas if they are to be successful. Rather than top management and the information department buying and imposing a new computer technology, for example, users have to participate to fit it to their purposes. People want involvement, meaning, and affirmation from their work, not just a paycheck.

Many managers spend fourteen-hour days trying to make hierarchical, individualistic organizations work. They sit through endless meetings trying to get departments to collaborate; they put out fires in one area even as they inadvertently light them in another. They commit themselves to visiting each employee every day.

Today, many executives have radically restructured their organizations. They have created visions to inspire employees, positioned divisions to serve specific groups of customers, eliminated layers to flatten the organization, decimated middle management to reduce bureaucracy, empowered people to make more decisions and be accountable, and developed teams that are supposed to be self-managing.

Yet even reform-minded leaders often presuppose rather than develop the spirited, rich, cooperative teamwork so necessary to make innovations work. They spend months fine-tuning their vision statement, but they do little to unite the workforce so that it can move toward its vision and serves its customers effectively. They create elaborate strategic plans, but they fail to involve employees and gain employee commitment to implement it. They give teams autonomy to make decisions, but they don't help them develop the effective relationships and skills needed to work together.

The Teamwork Imperative

Graham and his colleagues came to appreciate that productive relationships are needed to develop innovative visions, enhance corporate cultures, and forge adaptable organizational structures. The organizations of tomorrow must be created without a blueprint. No one knows what forms they will take. Teamwork is required to build our future organizations and make them work.

Graham and his associates also appreciated the value of cooperation theory as a foundation for leading. It clarifies important confusions about the nature of productive relationships. Leaders and followers are continually stymied because they are unsure how they should discuss their opposing views and deal with their frustrations. Cooperation theory provides them with a common framework of how they can lead, work together, and manage their differences openly to strengthen their teamwork.

Managers, especially middle managers, are often pointed to as the problem with our organizations. They are in between the strategic planners and the front-line people and thereby stifle innovation. The solution to this problem is to reduce their numbers and tell them to be facilitators. However, our organizations also need middle and other managers to become leaders, dedicated to developing and nurturing the cooperative relationships that underlie effective, adaptive organizations.

Learn Together, Work Together

Graham and his colleagues rediscovered that not only can leadership be learned, it *has* to be. Learning to lead is an ongoing pursuit, not the mastery of a few techniques or being born with the right genes. Leaders must be credible and must lead by example to show that they too are learning, if they are to fulfill their central role of developing people and the business. They too must learn and take risks, even as they ask, support, and cajole people to improve.

Leaders recognize that the status quo is an illusion, that change is relentless, and that organizations must adapt if they are to survive and flourish. In addition to modeling the way through example, they must point out that learning is necessary if they are to succeed and create opportunities for people to develop their competence.

Many organizations do not have much valued and invested in learning because they haven't seen results from it in improved job and organizational performance. The worlds of action and theory have too often stood in opposition. Professional education and training are too often carried out in classrooms and workshops far removed from the action of the boardroom and shop floor. Yet the demands today are too high to rely simply on trial and error learning. We need valid theory to guide our experimenting with leading and working together.

Graham involved the area managers and other staff at Cedar Lake Clinic in a joint learning cycle to understand and apply cooperation theory. As they together applied cooperation theory, each of them became convinced that the others were sincere in their commitment to developing these relationships, and that they had a common vision of the relationships they wanted. They gained experience and confidence that they could work together in cooperative, spirited ways as they discussed and decided how to work together more appropriately and effectively. The goal of cooperative work is also the means; the method reinforces the message.

Personal Growth, Leadership Development

In addition to bridging theory and action, learning and doing, Graham was also reconciling himself with his Cedar Lake colleagues. The tradeoffs between himself and his employees became less imposing and inevitable than he had originally assumed. He found he could advance himself as well as the clinic employees. Indeed, their aspirations marched together.

The essence of leadership is traditionally thought to be the authority to make decisions and the power to impose them. Many people shy away from taking leadership positions for they fear that others will consider them power-hungry, seeking power to compensate for some personal deficiency. Once they became a leader, they would be corrupted by power, they fear. A great deal of suspicion is directed at leaders.

But as we have seen, leaders do not *take* power from employees; they *help* people get needed resources and build up their confidence so that they feel empowered to perform effectively. Leaders help people develop the relationships needed to coordinate and combine their abilities to get things done and feel successful.

The beauty of leading through cooperation is that it melds self-interests, channels energy, and integrates ideas into mutually beneficial work. The challenge of cooperative leadership is that in today's marketplace, it must be done.

Leadership is noble, but it doesn't require self-sacrifice. Graham saw that he needed to nurture himself as well as others. For people to follow his lead, they had to know him as an individual and believe that he was personally committed to cooperative work. He had to communicate who he was, what his hopes were, and how he liked to work with others. People do not follow leaders who remain unknown and distant.

Graham was breaking out of the traps in the role of leader as he had earlier broken out of those of being a professional and a physician. He wanted to be a leader, but he also wanted to be himself. Rather than act out roles, he used the opportunities and obligations of leading to expand himself. He had to reach within himself as well as reach out to others.

Becoming a leader is a lifetime journey, not a destination. Leaders cannot expect or be expected to handle the challenges of leading perfectly and flawlessly. Problems and pressures are too great, and people are too complex and diverse for that. However, leaders can realistically commit themselves to learning, as they ask people to develop themselves and their organization.

References and Further Reading

This book is built upon the ideas and research of many people, some of whose work is noted below. Interested readers can use these references to explore their specific interests.

Teamwork in Organizations

Barrett, J. Why major account selling works. *Industrial Marketing Management* 15 (1986), 63–73.

Chase, R. B., and Garvin, D. A. The service factory. *Harvard Business Review* (July–August 1989), 61–69.

Coch, L., and French, J.R.P., Jr. Overcoming resistance to change. *Human Relations* 1 (1948), 512–32.

Cusumano, M. A. Manufacturing innovation: Lessons from the Japanese auto industry. *Sloan Management Review* 20 (1988), 29–39.

Eisenhardt, K. M., and Bourgeois, L. J., III. Politics of strategic decision making in high-velocity environments: Toward a midrange theory. *Academy of Management Journal* 31 (1988), 737–70.

Farnham, A. The trust gap. *Fortune* (December 4, 1989), 56–78.

Jackson, B. B. *Winning and keeping industrial customers.* Lexington, MA: Lexington Books, 1985.

Janz, T., and Tjosvold, D. Costing effective vs. ineffective work relationships: A method and first look. *Canadian Journal of Administrative Sciences* 2 (1985), 43–51.

Johnston, W. B., and Packer, A. *Workforce 2000: Work and workers for the 21st century.* Indianapolis: Hudson Institute, 1987.

Lawler, E. E. *The ultimate advantage: Creating the high-involvement organization.* San Francisco: Jossey-Bass, 1992.

Developing Leadership

Argyris, C. Teaching smart people how to learn. *Harvard Business Review* (May–June, 1991), 99–109.

Argyris, C., and Schon, D. *Organizational learning.* Reading, MA: Addison–Wesley, 1978.

Bass, B. M. *Bass and Stogdill's handbook of leadership: Theory, research and managerial applications.* 3rd ed. New York: The Free Press, 1990.

Congor, J. A. Leadership: The art of empowering others. *Academy of Management Review* 3 (1989), 17–24.

Hill, L. A. *Becoming a manager: Mastery of a new identity.* Boston: Harvard University Press, 1992.

Kouzes, J. M., and Posner, B. Z. *The leadership challenge.* San Francisco: Jossey-Bass, 1987.

Kraut, A. I., Pedigo, P. R., McKenna, D. D., and Dunnette, M. D. The role of the manager: What's really important in different management jobs. *Academy of Management Executive* 3 (1989), 286–93.

McCall, M. W., Jr., Lombardo, M. M., and Morrison, A. M. *The lessons of experience: How successful executives develop on the job.* Lexington, MA: Lexington Books, 1988.

Cooperation Theory and Research

Deutsch, M. *Distibutive justice: A social psychological perspective.* New Haven: Yale University Press, 1985.

Deutsch, M. Cooperation and trust: Some theoretical notes. In

M. R. Jones, ed. *Nebraska Symposium on Motivation.* Lincoln: University of Nebraska Press, 1962, 275–319.

Deutsch, M. A theory of cooperation and competition. *Human Relations* 2 (1949), 129–52.

Deutsch, M. An experimental study of the effects of cooperation and competition upon group process. *Human Relations* 2 (1949), 199–231.

Johnson, D. W., and Johnson, R. T. *Cooperation and competition: Theory and research.* Edina, MN: Interaction Book Company, 1989.

Johnson, D. W., R. T. Johnson, and G. Maruyama. Interdependence and interpersonal attraction among heterogeneous and homogeneous individuals: A theoretical formulation and a meta-analysis of the research. *Review of Educational Research,* 53 (1983), 5–54.

Johnson, D. W., G. Maruyama, R. T. Johnson, D. Nelson, and S. Skon. Effects of cooperative, competitive, and individualistic goal structures on achievement: A meta-analysis. *Psychological Bulletin* 89 (1981), 47–62.

Tjosvold, D. *Working together to get things done: Managing for organizational productivity.* Lexington, MA: Lexington Books, 1986.

Tjosvold, D. Dynamics of interdependence in organizations. *Human Relations* 39 (1986), 517–40.

Tjosvold, D. Cooperation theory and organizations. *Human Relations* 37 (1984), 743–67.

Conflict and Controversy Research

Deutsch, M. Sixty years of conflict. *The International Journal of Conflict Management* 1 (1990), 237–63.

Deutsch, M. Fifty years of conflict. In L. Festinger, ed., *Retrospections on social psychology.* New York: Oxford University Press, 1980, 46–77.

Deutsch, M. *The resolution of conflict.* New Haven, CT: Yale University Press, 1973.

Falk, D., and Johnson, D. W. The effects of perspective-taking and ego-centrism on problem solving in heterogeneous and homogeneous groups. *Journal of Social Psychology* 102 (1977), 63–72.

Johnson, D. W. Role reversal: A summary and review of the research. *International Journal of Group Tensions* 1 (1971), 64–78.

Johnson, D. W., Johnson, R. T., Smith, K., and Tjosvold, D. Pro, con, and synthesis: Training managers to engage in constructive controversy. In B. Sheppard, M. Bazerman and R. Lewicki, eds. *Research in Negotiations in Organization* 2, Greenwich, CT: JAI Press, (1990), 139–74.

Maier, N.R.F. *Problem-solving and creativity in individuals and groups*. Belmont, CA: Brooks/Cole, 1970.

Peters, Tom. *Libertation Management: Necessary Disorganization for the Nanosecond Nineties*. New York: Alfred A. Knopf, 1992.

Pruitt, D. *Negotiation behavior*. New York: Academic, 1981.

Smith, K., Johnson, D. W., and Johnson, R. Can conflict be constructive? Controversy versus concurrence seeking in learning groups. *Journal of Educational Psychology* 73 (1981), 651–63.

Tjosvold, D. Social face in conflict: A critique. *International Journal of Group Tension* 13 (1983), 49–64.

Tjosvold, D., and Johnson, D. W., eds. *Productive conflict management: Implications for organizations*. Minneapolis: Team Media, 1989.

Cooperation and Conflict Research in Organizations

Etherington, L., and Tjosvold, D. *Managing budget conflicts: A goal interdependence approach*. Toronto: Canadian Association for Management Accountants, 1992.

Richter, F., and Tjosvold, D. Effects of student participation in classroom decision-making on attitudes, peer interaction, motivation, and learning. *Journal of Applied Psychology* 65 (1981), 74–80.

Tjosvold, D. Rights and responsibilities of dissent: Cooperative conflict. *Employee Rights and Responsibilities Journal* 4 (1991), 13–23.

Tjosvold, D. Cooperation and competition in restructuring an organization. *Canadian Journal of Administrative Sciences* 7 (1990), 48–54.

Tjosvold, D. Power in cooperative and competitive organizational contexts. *Journal of Social Psychology* 130 (1990), 249–58.

Tjosvold, D. Making a technological innovation work: Collaboration to solve problems. *Human Relations* 43 (1990), 1117–31.

Tjosvold, D. Interdependence and conflict management in organizations. In M. A. Rahim, ed. *Managing conflict: An interdisciplinary approach*. New York: Praeger, 1989, 41–50.

Tjosvold, D. Interdependence and power between managers and employees: A study of the leader relationship. *Journal of Management* 15 (1988), 49–64.

Tjosvold, D. Cooperative and competitive interdependence: Collaboration between departments to serve customers. *Group and Organization Studies* 13 (1988), 274–89.

Tjosvold, D. Participation: A close look at its dynamics. *Journal of Management* 13 (1987), 739–50.

Tjosvold, D. Implications of controversy research for management. *Journal of Management* 11 (1985), 21–37.

Tjosvold, D. The effects of attribution and social context on superiors' influence and interaction with low performing subordinates. *Personnel Psychology* 38 (1985), 361–76.

Tjosvold, D. Power and social context in superior- subordinate interaction. *Organizational Behavior and Human Decision Processes* 35 (1985), 281–93.

Tjosvold, D. Effects of crisis orientation on managers' approach to controversy in decision making. *Academy of Management Journal* 27 (1984), 130–38.

Tjosvold, D. Effects of the approach to controversy on superiors' incorporation of subordinates' information in decision making. *Journal of Applied Psychology* 67 (1982), 189–93.

Tjosvold, D., Andrews, I. R., and Jones, H. Cooperative and competitive relationships between leaders and their subordinates. *Human Relations* 36 (1983), 1111–24.

Tjosvold, D., Andrews, I. R., and Jones, H. Alternative ways leaders can use authority. *Canadian Journal of Administrative Sciences* 2 (1985), 307–17.

Tjosvold, D., Andrews, I. R., and Struthers, J. Leadership influence: Goal interdependence and power. *Journal of Social Psychology* (1991).

Tjosvold, D., Dann, V., and Wong, C. L. Managing conflict between departments to serve customers. *Human Relations* 45 (1992), 1035–54.

Tjosvold, D., and Halco, J. A. Performance appraisal: Goal interdependence and future responses. *Journal of Social Psychology* 132 (1992), 629–39.

Tjosvold, D., and McNeely, L. T. Innovation through communication in an educational bureaucracy. *Communication Research* 15 (1988), 568–81.

Tjosvold, D., Meredith, L., and Weldwood, R. M. *Implementing relationship marketing: A goal interdependence approach.* Burnaby, B.C.: Simon Fraser University, 1991.

Tjosvold, D., and Weicker, D. W. Cooperative and competitive networking by entrepreneurs: A critical incident study. *Journal of Small Business Management* 31 (1993), 11–21.

Tjosvold, D., and Wong, C. L. *Cooperative conflict and coordination to market technology.* Paper, International Association for Conflict Management conference, Minneapolis, June 1992.

Tjosvold, D., and Wong, C. *Goal interdependence approach to conflict in the buyer-seller relationship.* Paper, International Association for Conflict Management conference, Amsterdam, June 1991.

Tjosvold, D., Wong, C., and Florence, L. Managing conflict in a diverse workforce: A Chinese perspective in North America. *Small Group Research* 23 (1992), 302–32.

Wong, C. L., and Tjosvold, D. Goal interdependence and service quality in services marketing. *Psychology and Marketing Journal* (in press).

Becoming a Team Organization

Johnson, D. W., and Johnson, R. T. *Leading the cooperative school.* Edina, MN: Interaction Book Company, 1989.

Tjosvold, D. *Teamwork for customers: Building organizations that take pride in serving.* San Francisco; Jossey-Bass, 1993.

Tjosvold, D. *Learning to manage conflict: Getting people to work together productively.* New York: Lexington Books, 1993.

Tjosvold, D. *The conflict-positive organization: Stimulate diversity and create unity.* Reading, MA: Addison-Wesley, 1991.

Tjosvold, D. *Team organization: An enduring competitive advantage.* New York: John Wiley, 1991.

Tjosvold, D. *Managing conflict: The key to making your organization work.* Minneapolis: Team Media, 1989.

Tjosvold, D., and Tjosvold, M. M. *Leading the team organization: How to create an enduring competitive advantage.* New York: Lexington Books, 1991.

Developing Leadership and Teamwork Skills

Johnson, D. W. *Reaching out: Interpersonal skills and self-actualization.* Englewood Cliffs, NJ: Prentice-Hall, 1991.

Johnson, D. W., and Johnson, F. *Joining Together: Group theory and group skills.* Englewood Cliffs, NJ: Prentice-Hall, 1991.

Johnson, D. W., and Johnson, R. T. *Creative conflict.* Edina, MN: Interaction Book Company, 1987.

Tjosvold, D., Tjosvold, M. M., and Tjosvold, J. *Love and anger: Managing family conflict.* Minneapolis: Team Media, 1991.

Acknowledgments

Becoming a leader is an ongoing journey of discovery and development that is too long and complex to do alone. Similarly, our preparation for this book began over two decades ago, and it has proceeded with the help of many colleagues and friends.

Developing, owning, and operating our family businesses have given us leadership challenges that forced us to reexamine easy assumptions and stretched our thinking. Our friends, colleagues, and employees have stimulated our development as leaders and have been full partners in creating our team organization. We have benefited a great deal from our leader support groups.

We have enjoyed working with many managers as they became leaders. Tom Brown, Pat Pratt Cook, Wanda Costuros, Bob Heywood, Jeremy Jarvis, Debra Keeney, and Bill McCourt in particular critiqued early drafts. Beth Anderson supported the book and contributed to its writing.

The book is built upon the work of Chris Argyris, Bernie Bass, Warren Bennis, Richard Field, Fred Fiedler, John Gardner, Bob House, George Graen, Rick Guzzo, Dick Hackman, Jim Kouzes, Ed Lawler, Mike Lombardo, Morgan McCall, Ann Morrison, Barry Posner, Vic Vroom, Phil Yetton, Gary Yukl, and many other capable leadership researchers. David W. Johnson and Morton Deutsch began and nurtured our appreciation of the profound implications of cooperative and competitive interdependence.

Margaret Tjosvold, our mother, has been a much valued business partner. We feel very fortunate that our parents and brother created a warm, loving family to grow up in. Jenny Tjosvold contributed to our research and writing and, with Jason, Wesley, Lena, and Colleen, has very much enhanced our family team.

DT, Vancouver, British Columbia
MMT, Minneapolis, Minnesota
March 1993

Index